WIDENER
BIOGRAPHY OF A LIBRARY

WIDENER
BIOGRAPHY OF A LIBRARY

Matthew Battles

THE HARVARD COLLEGE LIBRARY 2004
Distributed by Harvard University Press
Cambridge, Massachusetts and London, England

Copyright © 2004 by the President and Fellows of Harvard College
All rights reserved
ISBN 0-674-01668-8
Library of Congress Control Number 2004106842
Printed by The Stinehour Press in Lunenburg, Vermont

TO HARVARD'S LIBRARY STAFF
PAST, PRESENT, AND FUTURE
THIS BOOK IS DEDICATED
WITH ADMIRATION
AND AFFECTION

Foreword

WIDENER: A BIOGRAPHY. THE CHOICE OF TITLE WAS DELIBERATE, for Widener is so much more than a building. The structural edifice, formally named the Harry Elkins Widener Memorial Library, stands today in 2004 essentially as it did when first built by Eleanor Elkins Widener, her architects, and others who advanced a bold vision to give Harvard a library for "the College" while at the same time creating a lasting memorial to one of Harvard's sons.

Widener became animate in spite of its unyielding marble, steel, and brick. In its early years, certain rooms were filled with the bulk and seemingly unbounded energies of its young men while the sacred stack floors, in which the collections grew apace, were held apart for the true scholars, the faculty. The magnificent front areas of the library—its reading rooms, circulation desk, and catalog room—became well-trod spaces while the vast ten-level vault that surrounded three sides of the building remained, to most, a mystery. Staff worked in positions as defined and regimented as the architecture around them. But as the decades unfolded, changes in society and within the university altered the nature of Widener's inhabitants as well as the way they carried out their work. A constant backdrop to all these changes was the unyielding nature of the building: some chose to resist it, others to embrace it.

There is no way to know how many individuals' lives and careers were affected by working in Widener or to comprehend how many have made a mark on the world as a result of what they learned and discovered within its walls. How many authors, poets, and artists took inspiration from its collections or merely enjoyed a contemplative haven somewhere within? Did influential politicians, economists, social activists, or religious leaders emerge from the ranks of fractious men whose lack of discipline challenged those who managed Widener's reading rooms? And in later years, when Harvard's students were finally given access to the stacks, how many emerged from Widener better able to forge new directions for society, to pursue discoveries that would improve health, medicine, education, government, and science?

Every alumni reunion brings remembrances of Widener, many good, some not so good. Unhappy and frustrating memories remain for many, especially the women who for decades were not allowed to use Widener or were required to use it in very limited ways. Their memories cannot compare favorably to those who enjoyed the full privileges to explore the millions of volumes held within the stacks. Looking back, it does seem that each Harvard generation has experienced a different Widener in terms of how the library appeared either to welcome or resist students, to nurture or rebuff their inquiries. Widener has been a sanctuary to some and to others, a frightening maze.

In the pages that follow is a rich history of an entity that has indeed shaped many careers, leaving an indelible mark upon the long history of Harvard. In many ways it has been easier to write of Widener's more distant past, since there has been a longer accumulation of impressions to weave into a whole. It became more difficult with the recent decades, which compose an era of nearly tumultuous change in technology and in the expectations of users—users who have become increasingly diverse in their backgrounds and in the experiences that they bring to the library. Most who work in Widener today are, in many ways, too close to her subtle aging to determine exactly when certain changes occurred—or why. For example, the encroachment on Widener's public spaces came over a period of time, as did the persistent accretion of dirt and grime. Many, staff and users alike, had become inured to the dimly lit stacks, the sticky feel of the marble, and the loosely draped wires and cables that connected the old, venerable Widener to innovations of the latter part of the twentieth century.

Now, with the completion of a five-year renovation, that has all changed. Widener is revitalized. Once again, the beautiful and grand public spaces have been dedicated to the readers, whether they read books or work on their computers. We have used the building's architecture to welcome students, faculty, and other scholars into an array of services and to the magnificent collections still harbored in its ten stack floors. And above all else, we have provided a suitable environment for Widener's irreplaceable research collections.

This biography comes to end well before the life of this magnificent library shows any sign of drawing to a close. This nascent nonagenarian has had quite a past, but signs indicate an even livelier future lies ahead. Like most biographies, this one will leave some passages unwritten for others to pursue. And, as with any legendary entity, there will be a special cachet for remembering moments that do not appear within these pages. And just as we today have expressed our criticism and frustration with changes that were made by our predecessors, it is clear that history will be the real judge of all that has been accomplished through the five-year renovation and restoration of Widener Library.

Throughout the extensive renovations it has been our intent to prepare Widener for its second century of service to research and teaching. It is now, we believe, a library that welcomes readers and scholars and that accommodates the multi-faceted relationships among the library and the faculty, the departments, the institutes and centers, students, and the ever-changing world of scholarship. What will Widener be like fifty years hence? While no one can foresee the changes that will occur in technology, publishing, networking, teaching, and research, our hope is that Widener will prove as persevering, yet as resilient, as it has in the past. May future generations come through its portals, physical and virtual, with high expectations of the people and resources that reside within, and may they build upon Widener's many relationships with other libraries—within Harvard and around the world.

Nancy M. Cline
Roy E. Larsen Librarian of Harvard College

Preface

OF COURSE, I SHOULDN'T EVEN CALL IT "WIDENER." Eleanor Elkins Widener always wanted the library she built in her son's memory referred to as "The Harry Elkins Widener Memorial Library." She built it with her own money, after all, Elkins money. But "Widener" it has been to generations of Harvard students, faculty, and staff, as well as to scholars and visitors from around the world. Just as they make use of the books as they see fit to do, they take the lofty memorial and personalize it, make a friend of it (or an adversary, as the case may be). So in this sense at least, my book will not be revisionary–or rather, it ratifies a revision already long in the making.

As one who has worked in Widener as a librarian and a researcher, I know the peculiar influence the building exerts on its occupants. To those who labor within it, Widener is a presence, a personality, sometimes brooding, sometimes smiling. As a writer, I find myself less in a frame of mind than a mood which, though evocative and compelling, stands in the way of scrupulous, scientific history. As my title suggests, I have chosen to embrace this limitation rather than efface it.

Those who have worked in Widener during the recent renovation have likewise learned to live with limitations: construction barricades and closed entrances, changes in workplace and workspace. Now the project is over; the barriers have come down. And while what Nancy Cline says is no doubt true–it will be future generations who will judge the result–we can agree that, for those of us in the present, the end is glorious.

And if the impact and effectiveness of the renovation will be clear only in retrospect, it's for us now to look back, to understand our experience of the library in light of those who came before us. Renovations do this to us–they spin our heads around.

As you'll see, for the administrators and builders who have remade Widener, the work was as much a history lesson as it was a construction project. They have learned that past generations faced familiar challenges, and they responded in ways that both dazzle and puzzle us today.

Although the renovation is over, the work of understanding the library's history is far from complete. Widener's story is that of higher education in the midst of the social, political, and cultural tumult of the twentieth century; it is a story best told by more accomplished voices than mine. While I have followed the documentary tracks left by Widener's planners, directors, staff, and scholars, I have relied to a greater extent–perhaps too great an extent–on an intuition that is at once more personal and more literary than some may deem appropriate. The collection of library documents in the Harvard University Archives is a rich vein; if this book encourages others to mine that vein more fully and expertly than I am able to do, this will surely be its greatest, perhaps its sole, scholarly accomplishment.

For this is not a scholarly book. Despite my notes and sources and all my clumsy apparatus, it is a life that I have written here– the life of a library as seen from one vantage point, partial and intimate. I hope that those who know Widener better than I do not find it too impertinent, and that for those who have never known this library, or have known it briefly as students or visitors, it offers a vicarious taste of the thrill–and, no doubt, the frustration–this place gives those of us fortunate enough to frame our days within its walls.

Like the library itself–though to a far more modest extent–this book exists because of the efforts of many people. Peter Russell, Dan Craven, Darlene Smith, and their colleagues at The Stinehour Press have lavished on this project all the sagacity and aesthetic flare for which that firm is justly famous. I owe a hearty thanks to the staff of the Harvard University Archives–especially to Michelle Gachette, Andrea Goldstein, Robin McElheny, and Brian Sullivan, who made my use of their reading room a daily joy through many months of research. David Whitesell, collector and scholar of Harvardiana, shared with me a precious trove of Widener postcards, one of which is reproduced in this book. Contemporary photographs of Widener by Paula Carter, Jon Chomitz, Robert Ferrell Associates, Justin Ide, and Ron Tesler illustrate the last section; I am grateful for their hard work, as I am for the craftsmanship of photographers Robert Zinck and Steven Sylvester, whose portraits of books in the Harvard College Library are always exquisite. Monique Duhaime in Houghton Library made my life administratively easier in countless ways; Elizabeth Johnson and Josh Poupore in the Harvard College Librarian's office also smoothed the way for this book. Paul Bellenoit provided crucial insights and information regarding the renovation. A belated thanks is due Greer Allen, whose tuition in book design may have shown me the way to a bearable layout (the result is his as well as yours, Dear Reader, to judge). I am profoundly grateful to colleagues who agreed to read drafts of this manuscript at crucial–and frightful–points in its development: John Bethell and Brian Sullivan, writers and editors with deep knowledge of Harvard; my Widener-based colleagues Barbara Burg, Caroline Kent, and Lynda Leahy, who brought their experience of Widener as well as their acute textual judgement to bear; Houghton colleague Peter Accardo, a scholar of rare judgement and taste; and Ken Carpenter, whose understanding of libraries and their role in our history is without peer. Together, these patient readers offered a copious harvest of insights and ideas; had I been able to incorporate them all, the book would have been immeasurably richer. I owe an especially deep debt of gratitude to two colleagues and mentors: to William P. Stoneman, Florence Fearrington Librarian of Houghton Library, who prodded me to take on this project, and who then patiently gave me the time, space, and support I needed to complete it; and finally to Nancy Cline, Roy E. Larsen Librarian of Harvard College, who commissioned this book, and whose vision and editorial judgement have enlightened every page of the text.

Matthew Battles
Houghton Library
July 2004

Contents

vi   *Foreword*   by Nancy M. Cline, Roy E. Larsen Librarian of Harvard College

ix   *Preface*

1   *Part One*   DECEASE CALLS ME FORTH

53   *Part Two*   COLOSSUS

155   *Part Three*   MONUMENTALLY INVITING

185   *Postscript*

188   *Notes on Sources*

194   *Image Credits*

197   *Index*

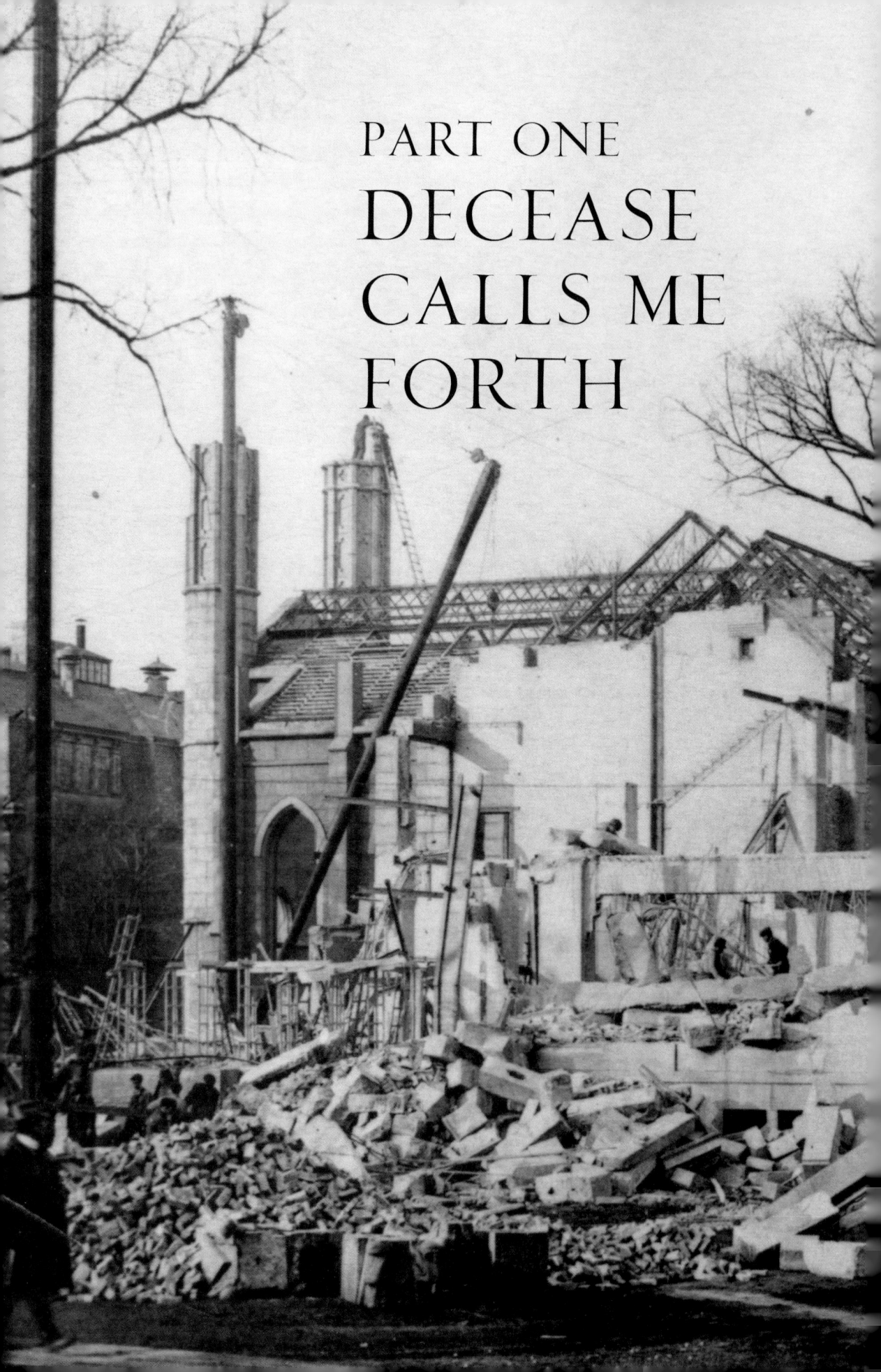

PART ONE
DECEASE CALLS ME FORTH

Above: *Harry Elkins Widener (1885–1912).*
Previous pages: *Harvard's own Gothic ruin: Gore Hall undergoes demolition in 1912.*

Since its opening in 1915, the Harry Elkins Widener Memorial Library has led a spirited life as Harvard's physical and, in a sense, its symbolic heart. Originally intended as the memorial to one man, in time it grew into a symbol of the life of the mind with few equals anywhere–and like all symbols, it has enjoyed its share of contest and contradiction. With its medley of neoclassical lines, federal brick, and massive scale, Widener's aspect at once recalls New England antiquity and signifies intellectual dominance. Its façade and its bulk in one stroke defined as a quadrangle what in earlier times had been a muddy field of hog pens, privies, and kitchen middens, bringing an elusive order to a landscape that bore the traces of three hundred years of Harvard's fractious history. With the construction of Memorial Church two decades later, the "New Yard" was framed by an architecture that acted out the university's aspirations: the spire of spiritual enlightenment on one hand, and on the other, the mass and weight of academic empire.

Yet while mournful beneficence, lofty ideals, and institutional ambition played their roles, they are far from the only factors at work in the life of Widener Library. The story of Widener is as much the tale of the students, staff, and scholars who used it as it is the record of benefactors and collections. In the life of a library so richly faceted as Widener, one dimension is as irreplaceable as the other. The life of Widener emerges from the archival traces of those people who worked in and used the library; in library rules and regulations; in the letters of students and staff; in the notes and reports of its caretakers; in the photographs and drawings of it, inside and out. Amid its products–the stream of publications, lectures, and courses that flow from it–traces of

Widener and its history are obscure. In our historical sensibility, libraries are transmitters, not subjects, of historical knowledge. Historian Alistair Black has called the library a transparent institution—its condition is that of medium, not message, and still less messenger.

Library history also disappears because of the mongrel nature of library work, which mixes the intellectual with the manual, labor with the liberal arts. From ancient Rome to medieval Europe, after all, librarians were called *custodes librorum*—the custodians or keepers of libraries, a vocation that mingles a scholarly sensibility with stewardship. Through the nineteenth century, even the largest libraries were so intimate in scale that the tasks of moving and shelving books were bound up in the work of controlling and classifying them. This mingling of the custodial and the curatorial can be seen in the life of Frank Carney, an Irish immigrant who began his Harvard library career as a stack boy in Gore Hall, the library that Widener would replace. When Carney arrived in May 1875, in the last full year of John Langdon Sibley's tenure as librarian, the library contained some 164,000 books; by the end of his nearly sixty-year tenure in the library, the total was well into the millions. In his career he shelved and reshelved, moved and moved again the college's ever-growing collection of books. In 1894, he helped move 15,000 books to Appleton Chapel, then moved them again when readers complained they couldn't find them. The following year he helped move 60,000 more books from Gore Hall to make room for much-needed renovations. Working so many decades among the books, Carney knew the collections perhaps better than anyone—well enough to help James Russell Lowell find in the stacks the books he had given to the library. Inspecting the volumes, Lowell complained to Carney about the library tags affixed to the spines. "I think Mr. Lowell is right from an aesthetic point of view," wrote Carney, "but as a matter of practical convenience the tag is a great institution." Carney's 1911 appointment as Building Superindent came just in time for him to oversee the move into Widener, and his thorough notes and reports are among the clearest windows into the life of the library in its early years.

In the middle of Carney's career, Harvard celebrated the turn of the century by conceiving a kind of time capsule. Called the "Chest of 1900," it was filled with memorabilia and personal narratives gleaned from some of Harvard's notable and long-serving characters. In his memoir for the Chest of 1900, Carney writes that he "was born in the country district outside the town of Drumore County Tyrone, Ireland on Sept 20, 1861 in a thatched roof hut such as is commonly used by the farmers throughout Ireland." His mother died in childbirth en route to America, and upon arrival in the States his father left him in the care of a widowed "grandaunt." In Cambridge, Carney lived on Appian Way. His neighbor did the library janitor's washing, dispatching the young Carney to deliver the laundry; on one of these missions, he was offered a job in the library. He left school with "great reluctance," and recounts how he nearly cried when he met John Langdon Sibley, who feared the boy might be "in consumption" on account of his "husky voice, [which he] mistook . . . for a symptom of that dread disease." He recalls that he already knew Sibley, as he and other school boys would frequently "waylay him" in the street to ask for copies of a paper devoted to humane treatment of animals called *Dumb Animal*. "Mr. Sibley was always glad to give us boys one of these papers," Carney recalls, "and would warn us to read it carefully and not throw it away." Once employed in the library, Carney earned three dollars a week as a page, and was given a fifty-cent raise in a couple of weeks. He entered service 17 May 1875; he was little more than thirteen years old.

As a page, his duties initially included fetching and shelving books–a job which, though entrusted to children, was among the most crucial in the library, as students could not enter the stacks to find the books they wanted. In addition to his duties in the stack, Carney brought the newspapers from Sibley's house to the office at 8:30 every morning and "wheeled coal for the furnace" after the library closed. He describes the method students used to call for books in Gore Hall:

> When the student found the card on the catalogue for the book he wanted, he left the drawer open with the card pushed back

and went to one end of the catalogue where a bell about the size of a dinner bell was placed.

He rang this bell and waited his turn[.]

When the "page" got around to him he showed him the card and the "page" memorized the title and number of the book[.] This was no easy task especially with some long German title[.]

I fear that I was guilty sometimes of coming back and saying a book was out when I had forgotten the title or did not see anything on the shelf that looked like the title I saw on the card.

Students ringing for help could be imperious with stack boys, Carney remembers: " [on] one such occasion when I reached the bell the impatient student grabbed me by both ears and gave them a strong pull. I was very indignant at such treatment and went to Mr Sibley and complained of him[.] Mr Sibley sent for him . . . and gave him a good talking to."

Carney also was sent to fetch books from Henry Wadsworth Longfellow's house. He writes that the poet "invited me into his study and then went and got some paper and rope to wrap up the books[.] He got down on his knees and started to tie the bundle[.] In my boyish conceit I thought I could tie up a bundle better than he and asked him to let me do it[.] "He arose from his knees saying as he did so that he guessed after all I had more experience tying bundles than he had."

On his own, Carney studied the shelfmarks and books to learn the arrangment of the collections, studied Latin with a tutor, and attended French, German, and English classes "in the evening high schools of Boston and the Y.M.C. Union." Long before Widener was built, Carney was well on his way to an encyclopedic knowledge of library collections.

By 1911, Carney had already worked for nearly forty years in the damp and drafty confines of Gore Hall. Built in 1841 after Richard Bond's Gothic design, fashioned from granite purchased from the quarry of President Josiah Quincy, Gore Hall expressed the fitful attention Harvard paid to European styles in the early nineteenth century. Facing Massachusetts Avenue, the building looked away from the prosaic brick of Harvard's workaday campus. As architectural historian Bainbridge Bunting points out, its setting also exhibited "a decidedly different system of paths, which encircle[d] the building in sweeping curves, entirely unlike the prim, efficient walkways of the earlier campus"—reflecting emergent ideals in American landscape design that would reach their apex in the work of Frederick Law Olmsted. This sylvan setting differed starkly from the more urban layout of both the campus and the rapidly growing city of Cambridge.

But Gore Hall expressed other ideals as well. In its Gothic style, with spires and a transept vaguely reminiscent of medieval chapels, Harvard's first library building tells us much about the meaning of the books it was built to contain. Gore Hall was not meant as a research institution so much as a secular chapel consecrated to the worship of the book, and its mystique transcended the confines of Harvard. So it seems to Henry James's Basil Ransom when he pays Gore Hall a visit in *The Bostonians*:

> [A]s he stood there, in the bright, heated stillness, which seemed suffused with the odour of old print and old bindings, and looked up into the high, light vaults that hung over quiet book-laden galleries, alcoves and tables, and glazed cases where rarer treasures gleamed more vaguely, over busts of benefactors and portraits of worthies, bowed heads of working students and the gentle creak of passing messengers—as he took possession, in a comprehensive glance, of the wealth and wisdom of the place, he felt more than ever the soreness of an opportunity missed; but he abstained from expressing it....

At the turn of the century, however, Gore Hall was symbolic principally of the library's troubles. As William Bentinck-Smith observed, "Gore Hall was a failure . . . . Its roof and windows leaked. Its cellar was damp and encouraged mildew. It was an enduring fire hazard. Its book spaces and arrangement were terribly awkward. Worst of all, it was soon outgrown and pronounced 'full' as early as 1863." Gore Hall's overflowing books and inadequate shelving forced staff and students into corners. In this, it was symptomatic of changes faced by libraries everywhere. "American libraries are growing far beyond the most sanguinary expectations," Justin Winsor noted in 1877, his first full year as Librarian of Harvard College. "When Gore Hall was erected, forty years ago, it was considered large enough for the accumulations of the rest of the century; but in twenty years there were calls for more space, and the least confident of us hardly expect that the century will go out without showing a capacity of shelves four or five times what was then contemplated filled to repletion." In 1877, Winsor pushed through a daring renovation of Gore, the centerpiece of which was the first book stack in North America—the now-standard shelving structure of iron girders that transfers the weight of the books directly to the foundation, rather than relying on the walls of the building for support of shelving. But even this addition was not sufficient; and by the turn of the century, the annual reports of Winsor's successor, William Coolidge Lane, were full of lamentations. "I have tried year by year to make plain," he wrote in 1903, "without exaggeration or concealment, the precise nature of the Library's needs, the dangers which attend a postponement of their relief, and the ends to which a wise policy would direct the Library's growth."

The trouble was not only burgeoning numbers of books, but the way they were organized on the shelves. Books in Gore Hall were still classified according to a "fixed shelf" system, in which call numbers referred not to a book's place in a scheme of knowledge (an approach most famously applied in the Dewey Decimal System), but to its location in a particular range and shelf in the stacks. In essence, the fixed shelf system was not so much a taxonomy as a geography, and the burden of classification rested not on learned cataloguers so much as on people like Frank Carney, who were the scouts, guides, and surveyors of the stacks. This condition gave Carney an inestimable knowledge of the layout of the collections; it also led to extraordinary exertions, since every addition of books required a revision of the classification scheme. In the face of very rapid growth, Carney noted, the system broke down, unless growth could be held constant across the classes, and if shelf space could be added at will—"and experience has shown," Carney wrote, "that both these conditions can be classed among the impossibilities."

Gore Hall's cluttered, atmospheric interior before the turn of the century.

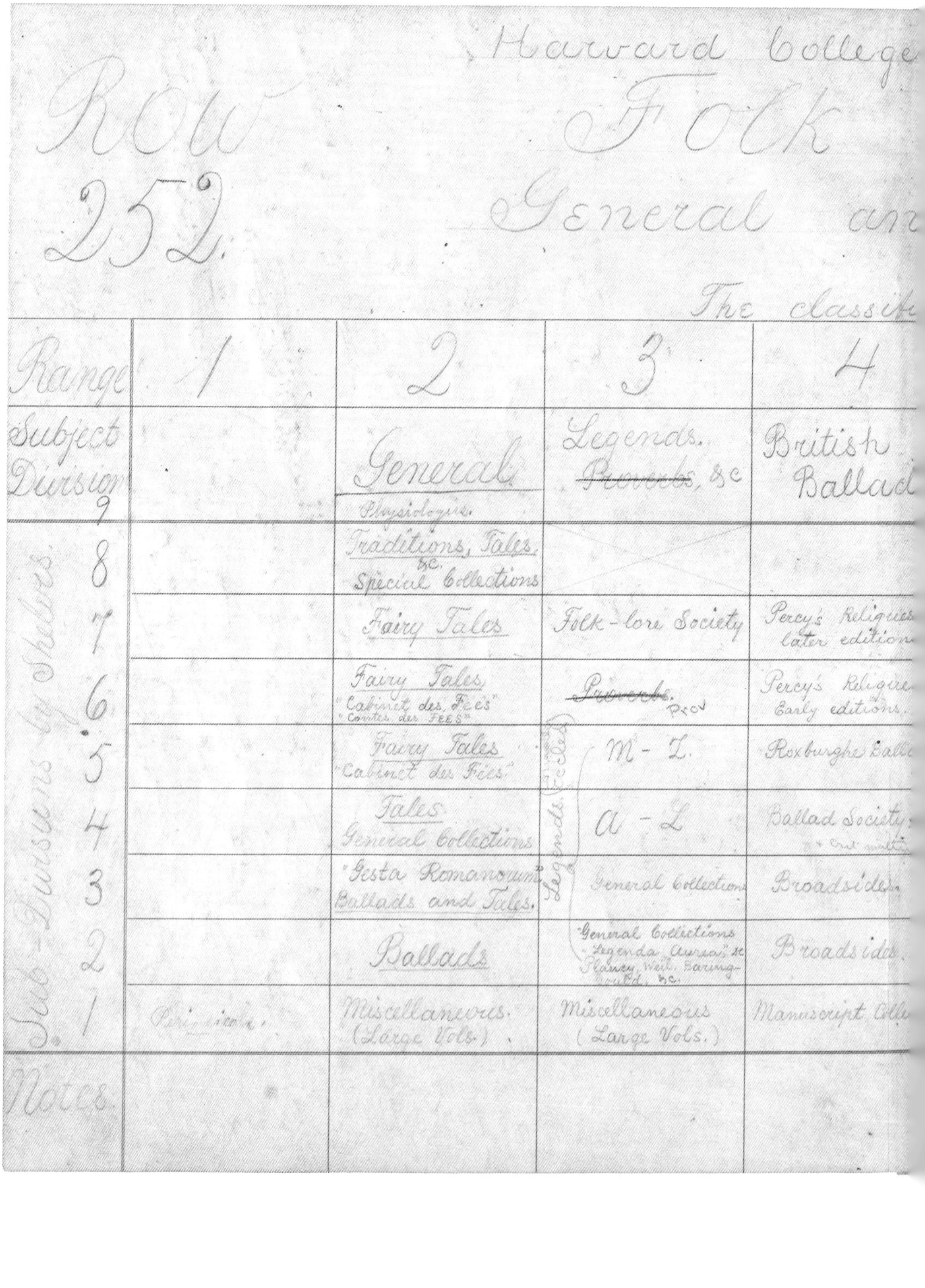

Harvard College

Row 252

Folk

General an[d]

The classifi[cation]

Range	1	2	3	4
Subject Division		General *Physiologus*	Legends, ~~Proverbs~~, &c	British Ballad[s]
9		Traditions, Tales &c. Special Collections		
8		Fairy Tales	Folk-lore Society	Percy's Reliques later edition[s]
7		Fairy Tales "Cabinet des Fées" "Contes des Fées"	~~Proverbs~~ Prov	Percy's Reliques Early editions
6		Fairy Tales "Cabinet des Fées"	M—Z	Roxburghe Balla[ds]
5		Tales General Collections	A—L	Ballad Society + one mo[re]
4		"Gesta Romanorum" Ballads and Tales	General Collections	Broadsides
3		Ballads	General Collections Legenda Aurea &c Flowy Weil Baring-Gould &c.	Broadsides
2	Periodicals	Miscellaneous (Large Vols.)	Miscellaneous (Large Vols.)	Manuscript Coll[ections]
1				
Notes				

(Sub-Divisions by Shelves)

(Legends cont'd)

Library Shelf-Guide.

Lore

Row

Germanic

on runs upward.

5	6	7	8	9
British Ballads	British Ballads	British Traditions, Tales, &c. ~~Proverbs~~	Dutch, Flemish & Scandinavian	Swedish, Faroe & German
Christmas Carols Metrical Tales	Humorous Ballads & Jests			"Volksbücher" Collections of Scheible, Simrock &c
Translations from the English & Individual Ballads	Humorous Ballads		Danish & Norwegian Ballads	"Volksbücher" Scheible, Kloster, &c
Local	Translations from the ~~main Scottish~~	Bibliography. Chap-Books &c.	Danish & Norwegian Tales, &c.	General Works Island Chroniken
Child's Collection Child Coll. (Boys)	Border & Local	Chap-Books Boswell Collection.	Norse & Danish Tales, &c. Collections of Thiele Rask, Asbjörnsen, Grundtvig	Scandinavian In general
Later Collections Nursery Rhymes	Jacobite and Later Collections	Chap-Books Boswell Collection	Norse & Icelandic Tales &c.	Faroe Swedish Ballads
Collections of Evans, Ritson, Percy, &c.	Collections of circa 1800 - circa 1850	~~Proverbs~~ Prov. Riddles	Icelandic ~~Norse~~ Sagas. Collections of Rafn, Arnason, &c.	Swedish Tales &c
Early Collections	Early Collections Ritual Works	Local Traditions Tales, &c. - Scottish	Flemish & Frisian	Translations from Danish &c. and Norse
Miscellaneous (Large Vols)	Miscellaneous (Large Vols)	Miscellaneous (Large Vols)	Dutch	Friesisch Volk — Literatur Local Lays

Two pages from Gore Hall's shelf list show the tightly nested complexity and collection-specific reticularity of the classification system.

William Coolidge Lane

Lane recognized that the shortage of space and cramped classifications deformed every aspect of the library's work. Scholars found it difficult to find the books they wanted; readers and staff shared their drafty, poorly lit, cramped rooms with piles of unshelved books; shelving troubles eclipsed consideration of other administrative challenges. "Whatever prevents efficiency," Lane continued, "either in the administration of the Library or in the use made of the books by scholars is a permanent loss, one that cannot be made up in the future. These are difficulties and shortcomings which are the most discouraging to grapple with, and give deepest concern to those who are the most interested in the College Library." Harvard would have to consider not only what kind of library it could afford to build and maintain, but what kind of library a university should have.

These challenges to the library reached their climax during the administration of Harvard President Charles W. Eliot. Beginning with his appointment in 1869, Eliot had turned Harvard, traditionally little more than a boarding school for elite youth, into a research institution of international reputation. He introduced the elective system in the undergraduate curriculum, promoted the professional schools, and placed a higher value on the research activities of his professors. His reforming energies boded well for the library at first, and Eliot considered various schemes for replacing Gore Hall. One plan proposed building a huge, tent-like wooden structure on the hillock where Houghton Library now stands to serve as a new reading room and administrative center, connected to the Gore Hall stack by means of a breezeway. Yet Harvard's institutional desires lay elsewhere. A committee convened by Eliot in 1902 to study Harvard's library problems recommended the building of a new library, but a lone dissenting voice, that of New York Public Library director J. C. Billings, argued against such a project. Not only did Harvard not need a *new* library, Billings wrote; it hardly needed a library at all. "The library should supply the immediate and important needs of students and teachers of the University," Billings argued; "it can never supply all their possible demands. . . . It should not purchase, and, as a rule, should not attempt to preserve books of this character which already exist in public libraries in Boston and are accessible to the professors and students of Harvard. . . . I think that Harvard University can use its present funds more wisely than in providing storage, cataloguing, etc., of rarely used books and I suppose that there are about 50,000 volumes of such books now in the library, which it would be wise to dispose of. The Library is much more in need of attractive reading rooms than of space for additional book storage." To other committee members—especially William Coolidge Lane, a longtime proponent of improvements in library space and funding—Billings's letter came as a shock. To Billings, Harvard's library was already too large—a bloated and overstuffed collection ill-suited to the narrow mandates of undergraduate education and scholarly communication.

Although it contradicted the findings of the majority, Billings's narrow interpretation of the role of the library in a university found favor with President Eliot and the Corporation. On 21 June 1904, Eliot wrote to Lane:

> As regards the future of the library, I think it is important that you should understand the frame of mind of the present Corporation. There is not a member of the Corporation that would vote to accept the gift of a new library building unless an endowment were also provided. If anybody should offer them a million dollars for a new library building, they would refuse it, unless the giver would permit the Corporation to erect a building of five hundred thousand dollars and keep the other five hundred thousand dollars as endowment. Moreover, there is not a single member of the Corporation who is converted to the opinion that it would be expedient for Harvard to maintain an immense, very comprehensive library in the College Yard. . . . So far as I can judge, the views expressed by Dr. Billings commend themselves to the Corporation more than the views expressed by the majority of the last committee. For the present, then, the policy must be the utmost frugality and no preparation for plans for a new building; and for the future the Corporation is determined to decline a building without endowment, and is not

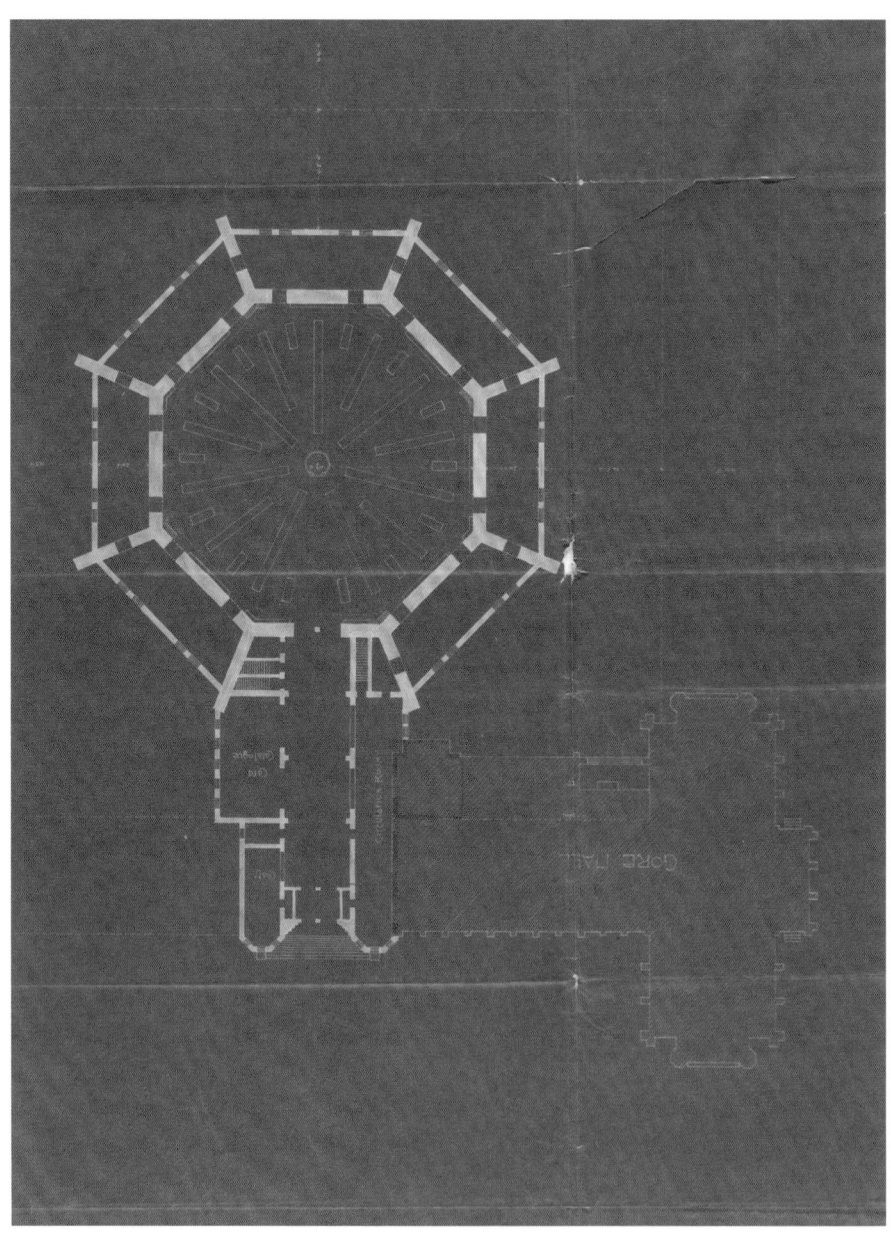

A blueprint rendering of President Eliot's abandoned plan for a great, octagonal reading room annex. Intended for the hillock where Houghton Library now stands, it would have dwarfed Gore Hall.

favorable to the general idea of a huge library containing millions of volumes in the College Yard.

And yet a decade later, Harvard would repudiate Eliot utterly, building that "huge library" with its "millions of volumes" in what would become the very heart of "the College Yard." What happened to change the Corporation's collective mind so quickly?

In that first decade of the twentieth century, vast changes transformed Harvard, the American library

Charles William Eliot

scene, and the world at large. At Harvard, Charles W. Eliot retired as President in 1909; his replacement, A. Lawrence Lowell, combined his predecessor's ambitious energies with an entirely different conception of the university and its role in society. In 1911, the New York Public Library opened its new main building at Bryant Park in Manhattan; an article in *Scientific American* that year praised the building for its ability to organize not only books, but people, into their rightful intellectual places. While New York's vast public library changed the meaning of books and reading in the metropolis, Andrew Carnegie's modest libraries flourished in small towns across the country. Everywhere, the gains of the Gilded Age raised up new institutions that sought both to benefit society and to manage its sweeping changes. Few places benefited from the new, activist philanthropy more than Harvard, whose endowment under Lowell would rocket from $22.7 million to nearly $130 million.

THE FORTUNES OF THE WIDENER AND ELKINS families were forged in the fires of industry that sparked and grew in the 1870s. While they came to active philanthropy later than the likes of the Morgans and the Carnegies, they followed the same trajectory; in retrospect, their ambitions have much to say about the elevating energies of the nouveau riche. Like many fortunes of the Gilded Age, the Widener money had distinctly modest origins. Born in 1834, patriarch P. A. B. Widener had served a brief apprenticeship as a bricklayer before switching to the meat business, opening in time a string of butcher shops. Civil War contracts to furnish the Union Army with meat expanded his business immensely, and after the war, he and a friend named William Elkins bought up and consolidated Philadelphia's streetcar lines. Widener took advantage of further opportunities to diversify his investments, buying into U.S. Steel, Standard Oil, and the American Tobacco Company at auspicious moments.

With his burgeoning wealth, P. A. B. Widener became an avid art collector, and as his family grew, they shared in his acquisitive zeal. His sons, George and Joseph, both collected assiduously; Joseph added decorative arts and rare books to the family repertoire. George married Eleanor Elkins, the daughter of his father's partner; their first son Harry, born in 1885, would make book collecting his specialty. While a student at Harvard, a sociable Harry found time to visit book dealers and ponder collecting; his first serious acquisitions, made in his junior year, were modest, and followed patterns typical of budding collectors of the time: illustrated books,

Harry Elkins Widener as "Mr. Butterworth" in the Hasty Pudding Theatrical The Lotos Eaters.

especially the works of Cruikshank, and first editions of nineteenth-century English literature. For her part, his mother both encouraged and abetted his newfound passion, making frequent gifts of books priced beyond Harry's students means: folios of the works of Ben Jonson and Beaumont and Fletcher, and Dickens manuscript items. Eleanor's attention to Harry's books would serve her well when she assumed their curatorship after his untimely death.

With the help of A. S. W. Rosenbach, a rising star among booksellers in Philadelphia and beyond, the Wideners refined their bibliophily, pursuing such rare and expensive books as Shakespeare's First Folio and the Gutenberg Bible. These rarest of books remained out of Harry's reach; even the family patriarch often found his wishes thwarted by the purchases of his acquisi-

Some books from Harry Elkins Widener's collection, including a small, beautifully-bound volume of the correspondence of Keats, vellum-clad works of social reformer and designer William Morris, and portfolios containing prints of Dickens Illustrator George Cruikshank and drawings by Thomas Rowlandson.

Decease Calls Me Forth

tive contemporary, Henry Edwards Huntington, whose zeal as a collector more than matched his vast fortune. Although P. A. B. Widener would eventually secure a First Folio for himself, the family would not succeed in acquiring a Gutenberg Bible until after Harry's death (though their copy would eventually join his collection in the Widener Memorial Room when it was given by the family to Harvard in 1944). Such rarities would remain out of Harry's reach even after Harry graduated from Harvard and joined the family business, when his new income secured his independence as a collector. Aware of the worth of his growing collection, Harry made out a will, naming his mother executor and bequeathing his books to his alma mater, "whenever in [his mother's] judgement Harvard University will make arrangements for properly caring for [them]."

Despite this premonitory arrangement, Harry continued to build a collection that he had every intention of enjoying for many years; as his mother would later recall, he hoped one day to build his own private library, and mused over which of his bookseller friends he would someday hire to manage it. Harry and his parents boarded the *Titanic*, which sailed from Southampton on April 1, 1912, days after he finished a whirlwind buying tour among the London bookshops, during which he purchased a number of books at the storied Quaritch shop, including a 1598 edition of Bacon's *Essais*, which he took with him aboard the ship.

While Harry was busy making his way in the family business and building his collection of books, his alma mater underwent sweeping changes, culminating in the retirement of Charles W. Eliot and the inauguration of a new President, A. Lawrence Lowell. An active scholar with specific ideas about the role of the university in society, Lowell brought to his presidency an ambitious agenda that would make Harvard international in reach and power. Eliot had aligned Harvard's resources with the national interest; in Lowell's hands, Harvard would become an empire unto itself.

At the same time, control of the library had been assumed by a professor named Archibald Cary Coolidge, whom Lowell appointed Director of the University Library in 1910. Solid and squarely built, Coolidge came to the library by a route that was as circuitous as it was illustrious: a renowned scholar of modern European history and later editor of *Foreign Affairs*, Coolidge had already pursued an active career as a diplomat and public servant, including senior posts in the American Legations at St. Petersburg and Vienna. His was a practical and worldly sensibility; as a scholar, he valued parliamentary minutes and local governmental records as much as rare books and manuscripts, and the structure of the collection he built at Harvard was innovative and far-reaching in its impact on the nature of scholarship in America. To Coolidge, management of the library was first and foremost about the management of books. It was through this bibliographically sensitive approach that Coolidge built not merely a library collection, but a library of collections—a massive, densely interwoven and interrelated array of books, pamphlets, and periodicals that could support not only teaching, but sophisticated research.

Coolidge had signaled this approach to library building with his first great gift to Harvard, the Hohenzollern Collection. Aware of the lack of resources in modern European history among American libraries, Coolidge set out to make for Harvard a collection that would do more than delight and instruct the polite student of German culture and history: it would instead provide the complete documentation of modern German civilization. There were fine collections of rare and interesting books both here and on the continent; Coolidge intended to collect not as a

Historian, diplomat, and library director Archibald Cary Coolidge, in a caricature by Ivan Opffer.

connoisseur and aesthete in search of ornaments, but as a hard-headed social historian engaged in the work of the world. And so he sent his agent, Walter Lichtenstein, in search of state documents, legislative minutes, local history journals—all the disconnected primary sources from which researchers might condense and anneal the story of a society.

Until this point, library collections were built in an entirely different way. William Coolidge Lane illustrated the ad hoc, casual nature of the library's collecting efforts in a report for the *Harvard Graduates' Magazine* in 1899. Lane describes "several interesting gifts" of collections received by the library, each covering a particular language, and each treated more or less as a curiosity. The first came from Mr. Leo Wiener, Instructor in Slavic languages, who "returned from his summer travels with a remarkable collection of Judaeo-German books. . . . The language of these books, a German dialect formed under Slavic and Semitic influence and printed in the Hebrew character, is of interest to the philologist, and the subject-matter of immense value to the student of popular literature and to the historian of the Jews. At the same time, information was received of another collection of books in the same dialect but printed in America, in the hands of a dealer in New Jersey."

Lane next mentions a small collection of philosophy books, and then another of foreign character: Pali expert H.C. Warren's collection of Asian texts, including the ten-volume *Japan Described by the Japanese* and a group of Sanskrit books. Warren and other Asian philologists could not rely on the library to supply them with a steady diet of books in the languages of their interest, for libraries at Harvard and elsewhere simply weren't collecting such things. Books from Asia were little-known, all but absent from the inventories of book dealers in the West, and exceedingly difficult and expensive to acquire. For this reason among others, Warren and his colleagues tended to be men of independent means, who could afford to build small, focused research libraries of their own, and who enjoyed the leisure time to hunt out other scholars and Eastern religious figures for help in finding the manuscripts and books they studied.

But this was about to change. At the turn of the century, immigration from Eastern Europe provided American intellectuals with an experience of multicultural richness on a vast scale. Of course, America had always been a polyglot nation of immigrants—but the Gilded Age philanthropists intent on bankrolling a boom in American higher education wanted scholarship that focused on the practicalities of commerce, labor, and technology. Such priorities would require vastly different libraries than those of the sort William Coolidge Lane and his colleagues had shepherded, with their mix of canons and curiosities. Walter Lichtenstein, writing to Coolidge in 1908, put it well: "[W]hat is more interesting than a collection on Austria-Hungary with its conglomeration of races, its variety of languages, and its manifold customs? It would be a unique introduction to historical, economic, and racial problems . . . . Hordes of emigrants are pouring into this country from Austria-Hungary, but there is not a single good collection of books relating to the dual Empire in the United States as far as I know." What Coolidge and Lichtenstein laid the groundwork for was nothing less than *Kulturgeschichte*– the thoroughgoing study of a culture.

But Coolidge and Lichtenstein were hardly the only voices of such change in American higher education. Ephraim Emerton, a Harvard Divinity professor with a vocal interest in the library, in an 1899 article in the *Harvard Graduates' Magazine* employed the latest metaphor used to describe the college library at the turn of the century: the library *qua* laboratory: "Especially the laboratory figure has been worked with great effect to show that the Library is no longer a mere storehouse of books, but a great workshop, wherein scholars of all grades, teachers and learners alike, have their places. . . . a university library should be not a mere book room, nor yet merely a combination of book rooms with great reading rooms where books are supplied to the mass of general readers, but that it must also serve as the daily workshop of those sciences whose material is necessarily chiefly to be drawn from books. To this end it must have a supply of small rooms, easily accessible from its book rooms, properly lighted day and night, where the teachers may carry on in their private studies and whither they can bring small classes of students for the consultation of books."

Emerton began by describing how little such space there had been in Gore Hall; when the stack was built, it was furnished with small tables at the ends of alternating rows, where a scholar "could enjoy all the heat from the floors below him and all the draughts from the floors above him, while all the conversation on all the floors, both above and below him, formed a pleasing accompaniment to his study." What he desired, by contrast, was a library that made room for scholars to work in proper quiet and seclusion, with room to keep books and materials together and to spread out their work. A thoroughly modern vision for the library, this—though one with ancient roots. And yet, what remains unmentioned is telling. In describing the "mere book room," Emerton did not consider the question of acquisitions—possibly because, for him and many colleagues, the choices were obvious and canonical.

At Harvard, it fell to Archibald Cary Coolidge to change this—and to change the canonical college collection into a research library in the process. The advent of such libraries would lay the groundwork for a transformation in which scholarship would cease to be the exclusive province of the leisure class, of those who could afford to build their own libraries suited to their specific needs. But with the research library came new mandates, new pressures, and new responsibilities, not the least of which would be to provide space sufficient to house the bibliographical needs of all possible comers—space for books of all kinds, space for a large staff to acquire and catalog them, specialized space for scholars to consult rare books, large books, maps, and materials in all kinds of media. With the construction of Widener, Coolidge would seize the chance to build his kind of library.

America's original political economist, Thorstein Veblen, would later describe the transformation of the American academy in darker and more critical terms. The "sentimental movements of the human spirit belong in the past," he wrote;

> the modern technology, and the mechanistic conception of things that goes with that technology, are alien to the spirit of

the "Old Order." The Church, the court, the camp, the drawing-room, where . . . elder and perhaps nobler virtues had their laboratory and playground, have grown weedy and gone to seed. . . . [T]hat power of aspiration that once surged full and hot in the cults of faith, fashion, sentiment, exploit, and honor, now at its best comes to such a head as it may in the concerted adulation of the matter-of-fact.

Veblen's vision would prove prophetic: through their newfound emphasis on pragmatic knowledge, universities would play a signal role in America's rise as the political, military, and economic hegemon of the twentieth century. Harvard would be in the vanguard of this advance—a role its libraries would help to shape and reinforce.

Yet Veblen also described the chief factor underpinning the success of the university: prestige. As universities increasingly saw themselves less as ratifiers of the good and the beautiful than as purveyors of essential information, they began to operate more like businesses—and increasingly, they traded on intangible qualities to position themselves favorably in the market of ideas. Like the Gilded Age economy at large, the modern university depended on a contradictory marketing program of nostalgic dreams and impossible expectations. One of the most telling symbols of that economy was the *Titanic*, whose glittering vastness concealed fatal inequities and inconsistencies. As one of the *Titanic* disaster's most auspicious products, Widener Library would similarly—albeit spectacularly and ultimately successfully—combine incommensurables: prestige and practicality, memory and prophecy, the liturgical order of old and the productive expectations of the new.

In many ways, Archibald Cary Coolidge was the paragon of the kind of university Veblen forecast for America's future, full of skills and knowledge of use to government and society. However senstive the scholarly and worldly Coolidge himself might have been to the social stirrings Veblen described, he also delighted in the day-to-day minutiae of what was in his time called "Library Economy"—the stamping of slips, the shelving of books, the granting of privileges, and the like. In a letter to Walter

Lichtenstein, written during a long diplomatic mission to China, Coolidge reminisced about a typical day in the library:

> If I were setting out a morning's work I should begin with you "Let me see, did you say you had made out that extra number in the Florentine history yet?–Oh, yes, of course, some odd moment when you have the time. By the way, have you taken out the Austrian books on the Reformation from Roman II and put them under Aus yet? I think that is worth doing as soon as you can. Yes, of course I know you are busy. Excuse me there is Miss McIntyre. Miss McIntyre, do you happen to have changed the cards yet on those books we gave different numbers to under Venice? You are quite right the works on the Reformation in Poland should be attended to first, and you remember that little batch on Russian history just after Peter the Great. Ah! There is Mr. Kearny [probably Frank Carney]. Good morning. Did I see John moving those works on German literature from the Architectural building? Prof. Franche [Franke?] would be glad to have them set up in their proper place. Now I must go for I have to tell Mr. Lane that I protest against having the books on India set up under anything but Dr. Dennis's new classification and first I must ask Mr. Kiernan to bind me a few more Slav. books, and repeat to Mr. Tillinghast that all the Hohenzollern and Chaucer volumes must have at least one card in the outside catalogue, and I must go upstairs to see if I can't hurry up the getting of the Skandinavian [sic] books into their proper place, and I want John to move a shelf or two for me, and I must see to it that Mr. Tufts has got that new map of Asia into the reading room, and Gray had it put up. When will you be ready to work out with me that new section of our Africa scheme? Oh! there is a man going to visit our South American collection, I must help him along, and there is another whom I want to persuade to help us out on our Indo-Chinese collection–Good bye." Such is the strenuous library life at Cambridge, Mass, USA.

Coolidge truly had an outsider's zeal, transitory and highflown, for the challenges of library management. His appointment usurped the professional control of librarians–in particular that of William Coolidge Lane, who had been unable to change conditions in the confining Gore Hall despite his frequent protests. Although disappointed by the effective demotion that Coolidge's appointment represented, Lane found in the professor a colleague as bent upon reform and improvement as he was–and someone with the administrative charisma to accomplish the transformation. When Widener finally opened, the two men would work side by side in the new stacks, helping library staff to heft the books into their rightful places on the shelves.

Coolidge's library ideals jibed with President Lowell's as well, and together the two men expressed a vision of the university library diametrically opposed to that of former President Eliot. In their Harvard, the library would be massive in size and far-reaching in influence, consistently acquisitive, and yet responsive to shifting intellectual currents. Coolidge and Lowell promoted the library energetically, building collections, securing funds, and campaigning to build a new home for the university's burgeoning collections. Years before the *Titanic* disaster, they were actively searching for a benefactor to build a great new library to replace Gore Hall. "When I cease to be President of Harvard College," Lowell wrote his cousin, the Revd. William Lowell, while in pursuit of a gift from J. P. Morgan, "I shall join one of the mendicant orders, so as to have less begging to do; and if mendicancy is a virtue, I have a right now to feel virtuous."

While Lowell pursued money for a new library, he told Coolidge to make plans and appointed a committee, which included Coolidge and Guy Lowell, cousin of the president and influential Boston architect, to pursue the question of a new library. Unlike the earlier committee of President Eliot, this one was expected to make definite plans for a new library building to replace Gore. The program they produced was at once ambitious and practical: by erecting, in stages, a series of stack buildings surrounding Gore Hall, they would create a "library quadrangle," effectively hiding the old building. Once the new wings were finished, Gore would be torn down, replaced by an administrative center connected to the new stacks surrounding it. When fully realized, their planned library would accommodate 2,130,000 books and would cost almost two million dollars—a high price in the midst of expensive changes Lowell was pursuing elsewhere across the university. Lowell's ambitious designs for a new system of undergraduate housing, which would replace the class-based quarters of old with houses that would mix incoming freshmen together regardless of wealth and social position, occupied the greater

Archibald Cary Coolidge at work in the library.

share of his talents and time as a fund raiser. And so despite Lowell's agreement with the plans of Coolidge and his library colleagues, there was no ready benefactor waiting to advance the library's prospects.

Then the *Titanic* sank, and everything changed. As the great ship went down, Eleanor Widener and her maid, Amalie Gieger, climbed aboard Lifeboat 4 alongside John Jacob Astor's wife, Madeleine Talmadge Astor; Eleanor's son, Harry, and his father, George, remained aboard. Their bodies were never recovered. Soon after her return home, Eleanor Elkins

Eleanor Elkins Widener

Widener wrote to Lowell notifying him of the terms of Harry's will, and of her attendant wish to build a small memorial library at Harvard to house her son's books. Lowell and Coolidge, however, angled for more. Hoping to convince her of the pressing need for an expansive new library, they sent her the library committee's recent report. Her interest piqued, Mrs. Widener invited Lowell to a meeting at Lynnewood Hall, the estate outside Philadelphia designed by the Widener family's favorite architect, Horace Trumbauer.

By the time Lowell boarded his train, word had gotten out to the press, and Mrs. Widener was not pleased. On June 12, Lowell wrote to her lawyer, John B. Stetson, offering apologies: "I am very sorry that Mrs. Widener has got a little put out with us. I am not surprised, as the reports in the papers naturally were provoking, and perhaps we also were too eager." Mrs. Widener at first felt that Harvard was asking too much of her. But Lowell, while courtly, was relentless, pointing out to Stetson that the resulting library, housing Harry's books and all of Harvard's, would be "the greatest collection of books in America . . . . it is hard to conceive

A. Lawrence Lowell

of a more enduring—certainly a more striking—memorial than that of a building to house our collections." Lowell went armed with Coolidge's figures regarding the expense of running the library, and a contingency plan: in case the project of a grand new library failed to attract Mrs. Widener, Coolidge drew up a proposal to build a new rare books library to house Harry's books and Harvard's collections of rare books and manuscripts. The visit went well, however, and Mrs. Widener committed to the larger library. In an undated letter to President Lowell, Mrs. Widener expressed her desire to move ahead:

> With regard to the deed of gift, of which we spoke when you were last here—I can talk it over with my lawyer when I get home & send a copy to you, if it is approved then you can sign it & send it back to me—Will you let me know if this is entirely satisfactory to you—

> In regard to the Press—please use your own judgement—the only thing I want emphasized is that the library is a memorial to my dear son to be known as—the "Harry Elkins Widener Memorial Library" & given by me & not his Grandfather as has been so often stated—

With a fierce dedication to her son's memory and an acute political intelligence, Eleanor Elkins Widener quickly made this grand project her own, commissioning the firm of her favored architect, Horace Trumbauer, to design the new building. A native of Philadelphia, Horace Trumbauer began his architectual apprenticeship in 1882, at the age of fourteeen. Opening his own practice in 1890, he soon found no shortage of clients among the nouveau-riche families of Pennsylvania's mineral and manufacturing sectors. In the nineties, he built many of the mansions that dotted the countryside outside Philadelphia. Not limited to elegant residences, his practice included schools, theaters, and libraries. He even worked on designs for an amusement park owned by the Elkins and Widener families, who soon became his chief clients. Despite Trumbauer's later decline in prominence—with his reliance on the neoclassical style, he was unable to adjust to modernism—the Wideners remained friends and loyal clients; when Trumbauer died in 1938, George D. and Joseph E. Widener served as honorary pallbearers.

While prolific, Trumbauer was eclipsed in the twentieth century by modernist architects who eschewed his classical bent. His most interesting and innovative decision, perhaps, was to hire Julian Francis Abele, one of the first African-Americans to hold an architecture license and a draftsman and designer of considerable talent. In ironic contrast to his mentor's humble and practical apprenticeship, the young Abele had acquired elite training and impeccable credentials. A brilliant and energetic student whose commencement address at the Institute for Colored Youth was entitled "the Role of Art in Negro Life," he was the first African-American graduate of the architecture program of the University of Pennsylvania. He honed his draftsmanship and aesthetic sensibility in France, where he sketched architectural monuments and probably attended classes at the Ecole des Beaux-Arts. Upon his return to Philadelphia in 1906, he joined Trumbauer's firm, where he would remain for most of his career. Although Trumbauer relied on Abele's brilliance, the latter was little known outside his Philadelphia circle; not until his mentor's death in 1938 did he so much as sign his own work. The American Institute of Architects failed to elect him to membership until 1942; in all likelihood, his race was a factor. While it is not clear what role Abele might have played in the design of Widener, it is likely that he took part; and Dreck Spurlock-Wilson's *African-American Architects: a Biographical Dictionary* (2004) lists Widener among the many buildings which Abele helped to design over his long career.

News of the proposed library was greeted by Harvard faculty with enthusiasm—and no small amount of politicking. Ephraim Emerton wrote to Coolidge in a tone that cast fond hopes in the form of sage advice:

> My dear Coolidge, This is a letter of congratulations to you and myself and all the rest of us on the glorious news I have just been reading in the *Transcript*. After hoping against hope for a life-time, it seems too good to be true that we are really going to have a Library!—and that it will be a new building and not a shabby reconstruction of Gore Hall is best of all. The Transcript account is probably as inaccurate as usual, but making all allowances, the prospect remains alluring to a degree. The next two years will naturally be a period of chaos, but we shant mind that.
>
> My only worry comes from my ineradicable distrust of all architects—a distrust which the history of Harvard building certainly

goes far to confirm. Is it going to be possible to have the plans submitted to the criticism of a variety of persons, especially persons who have had experience in the actual use of libraries? Most of our Harvard building abortions [?], such as the Fogg Museum, New Lecture Hall, Divinity Library have resulted from failure to seek such criticisms—while the successes—Robinson and Emerson for example—come from careful consultation with those who were to use the buildings.

Are you perfectly clear as to the wisdom of a great big reading-room? It is a pleasure to think that our department is going to have a worthy looking [building?] commensurate with its importance, and also that the idea of a library as a work-room seems at last to have penetrated even the Harvard Corporation.

My share will be but small and brief, but my joy for those who are to have this splendid equipment is none the less complete.

I wish, where the question of arrangement comes up, that the subject of restoring "Theology" to its proper place could be reconsidered de novo. In any case, put me down as insisting that the deposition of any "Theology" which can be separated from all science, shall be restricted to the narrowest possible limits.

Harvard had no shortage of other experts, of course, such as Benjamin Rand, librarian of the Philosophy Department, who in a letter to President Lowell asserted his own magisterial command of library economy:

> As a University always has a just claim to the best thought of its officers, kindly permit me to state without elaboration as the result both of experience and observation two principles that appear to me to be essential in regard to a new University Library.
>
> First: The future university library must I am thoroughly convinced embody throughout the principle of departmental libraries. This principle I have developed in the Nation of March 24, 1907 and need here state that it implies only such knowledge and administration of special departments as has given prestige to the Harvard Law Library. It has also been adopted with success in several departments of the New York Public

> Library. Its complete application would ensure not merely an enlarged storehouse, but also a correct basis for all future development. Such a method would permit of unlimited growth, and its ultimate adoption might thus largely compensate for the prolonged delay in past construction.
>
> Secondly: A university library ought also to be made as far as possible a centre of academic instruction and especially one for the guidance of productive work. For this purpose it ought to have not merely as at present an administrative staff, but also an academic one. The heads of the several departments into which the library would most wisely be divided might it seems to me form this chiefly academic library board, and be made up chiefly of the faculty best qualified to direct and inspire the work in the library for these various divisions.

While faculty received news of the new library warmly, the staff in Gore Hall began making preparations for their move. Their quixotic plan was to keep the library open and accessible throughout the construction of its new home; both books and staff would need space that was safe for books and convenient for readers. Through careful diplomacy, Coolidge sought temporary housing throughout the Yard. He knew that the challenges were not only administrative, but political: "I am afraid I shall have to ask for almost arbitrary powers in such things as where the books will be stored," he wrote to Lowell in June 1912. "Of course, I do not want to be autocratic wherever I can possibly avoid it . . . but the thing has got to go as a great machine which cannot be delayed in its parts by argument." Coolidge faced myriad options, none of them ideal: a temporary building behind Massachusetts Hall was proposed; the option of moving the whole stack of Gore Hall east towards the President's house–today the site of Lamont Library–was briefly considered as well. The space under the bleachers at Memorial Stadium was large enough to accommodate almost all of the books. He consulted chief of Harvard Athletics L. B. R. Briggs, who wrote back in the affirmative: "If the people who use the library can stand the inconvenience of a stack in the Stadium, the (Harvard Athletic Association) should be able to stand it. Of course . . . the games would go on as usual. On certain afternoons there would be noise . . . ." Andover

Library agreed to accept 50,000 volumes, most of them theology, and Coolidge exerted pressure on various schools and departments to accept stocks of books their faculty used. Then he hit upon the plan of using Randall Hall–a student dining space, then vacant–to house the majority of the books, as well as space for staff and services. This decision proved most workable, and was accepted–though Coolidge still took delight in the notion of a library in an athletic arena, later writing to Lowell, "I should like to have seen Channing's smile when he heard that he would probably have to write the next volume of his great work under the Stadium."

In September 1912, students and faculty returning to campus learned that Gore Hall would be evacuated immediately. With temporary repositories identified, the books began to move–first in a trickle, soon in a freshet–out of the old library. Frank Carney's shelvers and assistants worked quickly; no doubt the many shifts of books in Gore as the collections outgrew their space had trained them to move books with dispatch. "The next problem," he recorded in his report, "was to construct the shelving and move the books at the same time. . . . As the floor irons in Gore Hall were used in the floor construction it wa[s] necessary to plan the moving so that the rows with the proper width should be emptied first. This naturally led to the placing of subjects side by side that had little relation to one another."

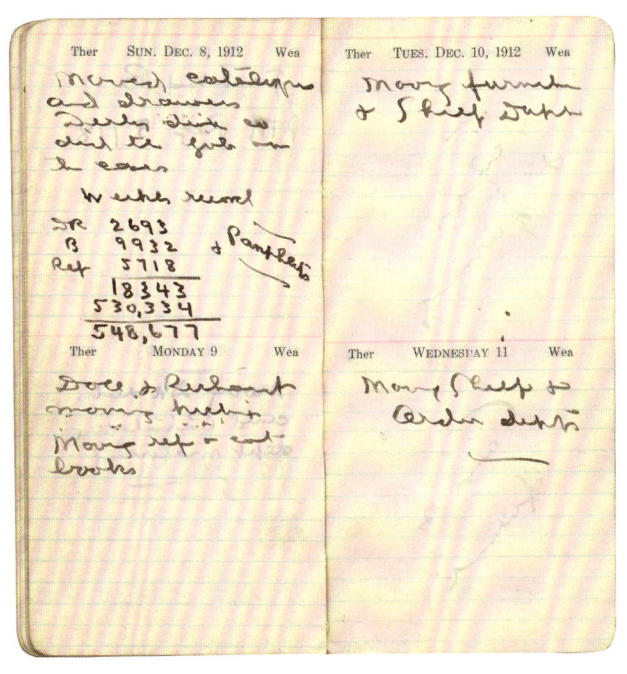

Frank Carney's diary records the movement of books, staff, and supplies out of Gore Hall in 1912.

Despite the commotion and confusion, Carney found time to

Carney's "automobile truck" and book slide in operation removing books from a Gore Hall bedecked with incongruous awnings.

document the move to Randall Hall, nearly book-by-book, in a small calendar diary he acquired expressly for the purpose. The first entry for 20 August 1912, records only some modest shifting. On Wednesday, 21 August 1912: "Moving Gore Hall books from stacks." Gore Hall's alcoves were emptied in three days, but these were only a warm-up for the real business. Folklore and Emblems, totaling 12,625 books, were moved together in a day and a half. In the next month, shifting proceeded apace: by 21 September, Carney records a total of 139,056 books moved, with 37,383 making the journey in one especially active week (Coolidge had cautiously hoped for a high mark of ten thousand per week). Through October and November, the big classes—French History, English Literature, and British History in one week, US History, Philology, and Classics the week following—at the rate of more than one hundred thousand books a week, finishing in December with a total of 548,677 volumes moved from Gore to Randall Hall.

For a building superintendent now absent a building, Frank Carney was a busy man. His report for 1912 makes clear how efficiently and systematically the moving process had gone forward. "Long wooden boxes about four and a half feet long by fourteen inches in width and nine inches deep were used," he writes. "A load consisted of twenty-four boxes. These boxes were numbered from one to twenty-four and were carried from the building in an auto truck . . . . [M]ovable wooden shutes were erected from the upper floors to a raised platform so that it was possible to slide the boxes directly into the automobile by their own weight." At the final destination, the process was reversed, and the books now proceeded up an incline: "In Randall Hall a cable was used, with a pair of trolley wheels attached to a strong oak board with iron hooks to fasten the boxes so that they could be hoisted to the various floors. By using the various devices the movers were never obliged to go up or down stairs and they were able to move the books with less labor and more rapidly."

The automobile truck used in the moving of the books would be employed throughout the library's exile, delivering requested volumes to readers from their scattered locations throughout the

Yard. The newfangled conveyances made an astonishing appearance in the Yard, albeit a quiet one—for they were electric automobiles, the batteries of which were charged nightly in a specially built garage tacked onto Randall Hall. The efficient vehicles soon were delivering books as well as parcels in the new interoffice mail service, which Carney also pioneered. "Auto Delivery . . . made it possible to get any book neede[d] within half a day under ordinary circumstances, and at once in emergency cases [!]." Readers could even get books while the library was on the move: "No books were inaccessible except while in transit on the auto truck. In some cases a book wanted was in the packing box at either end was taken out and delivered directly to the borrower. . . . While naturally there [were] some difficulties in the prompt delivery of books," Carney admitted, "on the whole the system worked very satisfactorily." He promised that the "auto delivery will be kept up during the scattered condition of the library."

Carney, of course, was hardly the only staff member to work on the move, nor were books the only part of the library in need of moving. In addition to a host of workers hired especially for the effort, the library's regular staff played an active role. "Sunday [7 December 1912] was a very busy day for the male force of the library," Carney recorded. "The catalogue cases were moved and set in place. . . . That 3382 drawers were moved withou[t] the spilling of a single drawer or damage of any kind shows how well this job was handled. It was hardly expected that this work could be done in one day. . . . With the catalogues in place the most difficult part of the staff moving was done. On Monday morning [8 December] the catalogue and delivery departments started work on Monday at Randall Hall without any loss of time. The Shelf and Order departments were moved on Tuesday and Wednesday, thus completing the staff moving."

With his customary thoroughness, William Coolidge Lane recorded for *Library Journal* how the Harvard College Library was made to fit into a dining hall:

> The serving-room along the north side of the building is occupied by the order department and the shelf department. The scullery accommodates the cataloging staff. . . . After some shift-

ing of partitions, the "student waiters' dressing room" becomes the librarian's outer office and the registrar's office; a small room, called a "dormitory" on the old plans, is turned into the librarian's office, and another "dormitory" is occupied by typewriters. Typewriters also are placed in the "pastry and ice-cream room." Below in the kitchen, the ranges have been boarded up, though the big red soup cauldrons may still be seen, and the room gives ample space for unpacking boxes of books, collating them, putting in seals, etc., while the dumbwaiters going up to the shelf department, just above, are a luxury we never knew in Gore Hall.

A bakery, cut off from one side of the kitchen, makes a capital bindery. A large space in the basement, divided off by netting and formerly used for "dry stores," is the newspaper room. The potato room, with its brick walls and hard cement floor, newly whitened and shelved with the sliding cases from the Treasure Room in Gore Hall, makes a safe depository for our rarest and most valuable books. There are refrigerators in bewildering variety, some of which are used for storing boxes of books before they are unpacked, and in one of which we may put the books of the "Inferno."

Randall Hall's cold storage seems especially appropriate for the "Inferno" books; named after Dante's disturbing comedy, the Inferno case held books deemed too "hot" for delicate undergraduate sensibilities and thus kept locked away in a cabinet. In Widener, the Inferno case would become infamous for holding not only the dark, the violent, and the pornographic as well as the more academically respectable and yet still titillating works of Freud, Kraft-Ebing, and other pioneer students of human sexuality.

While Carney and his crew muscled the books into place in Randall and elsewhere, Lane and Coolidge wrestled with the challenges posed by scattered books, staff, and readers, meanwhile conceiving the shape the library would take inside its new home. They were swamped with choices, deluged with the letters and circulars of eager contractors, and hampered by the subtle politics at play among donor, architect, and administration. Lane's letters show his attempts to make the new library work as an idea factory. The latest bookstacks in vogue at other libraries were technological wonders, laced with numerous booklifts and conveyor belts to shepherd the books to the reading rooms, and with dense networks of telephone stations to alert pages to readers' needs. Lane and Coolidge hoped that they could provide something similar in their new library. "The only system which I can conceive," Lane wrote to Trumbauer, " . . . is a continuous belt with carriers going up + down on each side at a convenient point in the E+W stacks + either under (through the basement) or over, crossing in a conduit from on the level of the top story or even above it." Lane's letter makes clear how precisely he and Coolidge planned the flow of books in the stacks; the whole design would reflect the model of a closed stacks with books fetched by runners, not readers.

The plans Trumbauer submitted, meanwhile, similarly reflected the library's catholic purposes and its traditional conception. Work places for scholars and staff were distributed throughout the public regions of the building; scrupulously differentiated, sites of work and repose were as rigidly segregated according to the social scale. There was a vertical segregation as well, in which basic functions and the lives of staff members were relegated to the ground, the first floor given over to reception of the public, and the upper floors devoted to higher pursuits of reading and research. On the ground floor, staff space was divided into separate locker rooms for men and women, a women's dining hall, and a locker room and dining hall set aside especially for "boys." The "scrubwomen" were given a room of their own as well, complete with toilet and lockers, separate from that of the other women. The headquarters of the shelf department was placed on the ground floor, along with space for collation, receiving, duplicate book storage, and offices. Contravening the otherwise rigid hierarchy of upstairs and downstairs, the ground floor did contain one massive reading room set aside for government, history, and economics. This, however, principally gave access to course books on reserve, and so was designed for undergraduate use. Only ten studies were sited on the ground floor, which contained none of the cubicles for graduate students that punctuate the stacks on higher floors. The first floor contained the major administrative suites, with offices for the Director and the Librarian, as well as workrooms for acquisitions and cataloguing. The Treasure Room, the University Archives, and the Quinquennial Catalogue Room were special spaces; the faculty had their own coatroom and toilet (now the men's and women's rest rooms in the staircase area). Trumbauer's plans gave over the second floor to the fetching and reading of books. The card catalogue enjoyed a pillared space of its own, beyond which lay the delivery room, which guarded the end of the east stack; next to it was nestled the tiny Radcliffe Reading Room, barely large enough for a single table. (In the finished building, this women's reading room was quartered in an equally small space on the other end of the second level; in more recent years, both areas have served as offices.) The Main Reading Room, where women were not under normal circumstances allowed, ran the width of the building. Above this level, more specialized reading rooms were planned, including a room for art and architecture, a map room, and a photograph room. When Widener opened, the Harvard Business School Library and the Theatre Collection would occupy large areas of the third floor, though this is not reflected in Trumbauer's submitted plans.

While Coolidge and Lane conceived of the library as a storehouse for books, Trumbauer designed with aesthetics rather than utility in mind. His vast entrance hall, stairs, and ornate reading rooms remained the centerpieces of the building, and the architect was loath to spend limited funds on those parts of the construction unlikely to enjoy public display. Coolidge complained to Lowell in a memo dated November 6, 1912:

> In the discussions so far the difficulties have been to settle satisfactorily three main points,—first, the number of studies and cubicles; second, the amount of stack space; third, the quarters for the staff and the various special rooms. If the architect is able to provide for the minimum requirements on which we are insisting, we can accept his plan as eminently satisfactory and feel nothing but gratitude. What we wish for is:

First, 80 studies and 350 cubicles.

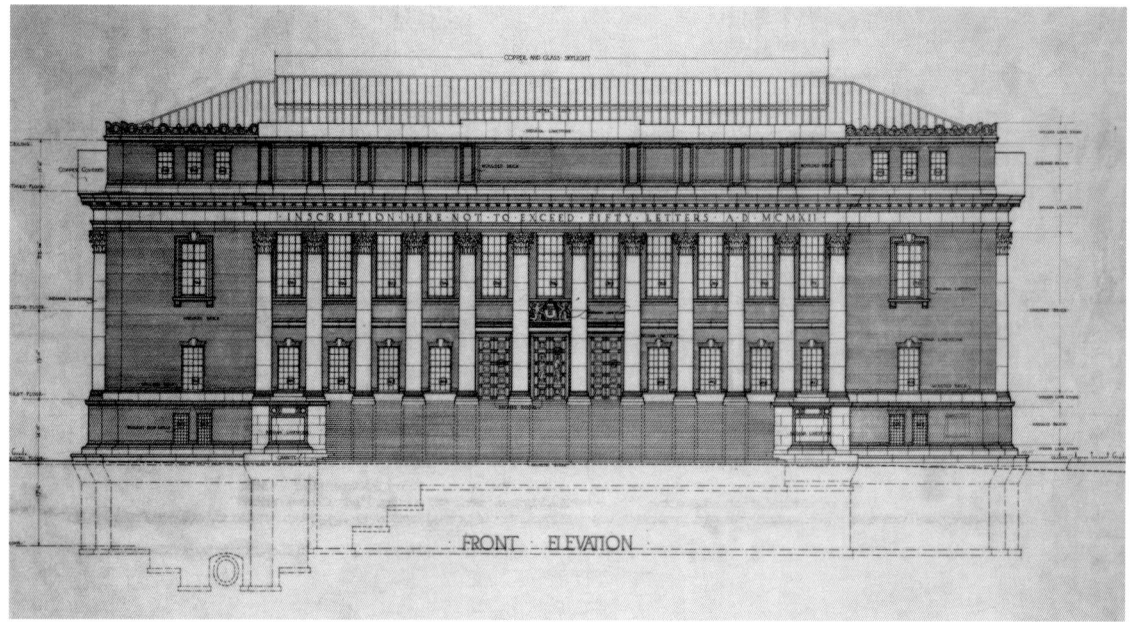

> Second, stack space (as technically counted) for 2,500,000 volumes, and this without counting what may be put along the walls of certain rooms or the space necessary for a newspaper collection, and without sacrificing space in the basement necessary for many miscellaneous purposes.

> Third, the plans last presented, with such modifications as were approved by Mr. Lane in his last visit to Philadelphia, may be accepted as adequate to the needs of the staff and the administration of the library, and to the department and other special rooms, but no further encroachments on this space should be made, for it is not abundant now.

Lane, meanwhile, persisted to raise questions about plans for the stack, which he saw as the heart of the library. As fliers from manufacturers far and wide piled up on his desk—his papers in the Harvard Archives include trade cards from firms selling trash compactors, heating systems, and "Royal Flush" toilets—Lane contacted librarians across the country for advice on the latest stack designs. Some could barely contain their envy at the size of the Widener gift. C. W. Andrews of Chicago's John Crerar Library expressed his good wishes with a barely disguised chagrin: "[A]n acquaintance who was an intimate friend of the family + the donor has told me of the gift and its amount. It seems probable that you will not have to consider economy as closely as we shall."

As Lane researched possible designs for the stack shelving—including systems using ratchet drives to adjust the level of the shelves—he met continual frustration in the form of Trumbauer's inattention to the needs of the backstage, so to speak—to that hidden-away stack of books that his neoclassical design would hold as dearly as a fistful of coins. When a revised set of plans arrived

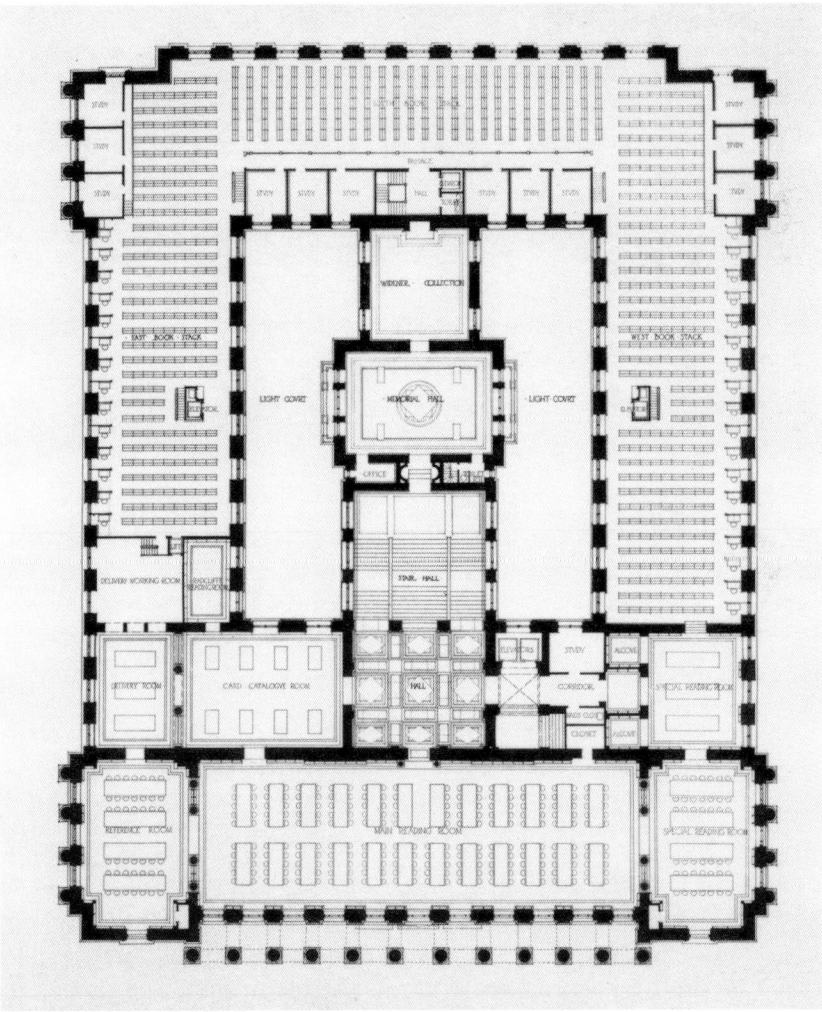

Opposite: *Trumbauer's Massachusetts Avenue Elevation, with a cherubim-laden tablet over the door and the legend "inscription here not to exceed fifty letters . . . ."* Above: *Floor plans for Widener's second level show the placement of studies, work rooms, and memorial spaces, the extent of the stacks, and the disparity in size between the main reading room and the tiny space alloted to Radcliffe students.*

Above: *Widener Library rises in the Yard.*

with stack space shorted and Lane's proposed system of elevators conspicuously absent, the librarian complained to Coolidge:

> The plans will be severely criticised on account of the position of the Delivery Room, which is thirty-two feet above the level of the ground and at a considerable distance from the entrance. We ought to counter-balance this by bringing the elevator as near as possible to the door and as near as possible to the Delivery Desk. The man who makes his way to the Delivery Desk on foot has first to climb thirty-two steps outside (13 feet high), walk 92 feet from the top of these steps to the foot of the stairs, go up 22 steps (11 feet) to the platform, turn and go up 16 steps more (8 feet) to the hall, from which it is 86 feet to the Delivery Desk. This means going up to the height of the sixth floor of the stack in our old building and walking twice the length of Randall Hall, in which the Library is now established. It seems to me imperative to make the elevator as accessible and convenient as possible.

At the same time he and Coolidge, recognizing the historical significance of the the shelving now being stripped from the bowels of Gore Hall, hoped to retain a section of the old stack and to preserve it in the new library. Trumbauer nixed this, meanwhile reducing shelf supports, shortening aisle lengths, and reducing the number of carrels and studies throughout the stack—all in an attempt to conserve dwindling monies. He preferred instead to spend on limestone and carved Italian marble. Coolidge and Lane fought back, however, complaining to Lowell that changes to the plans would produce a beautiful but unworkable library. With Lowell's intervention, and Eleanor Widener's blessing, stack space was restored and reorganized along library standards; Trumbauer compromised on carrels and cubicles as well. Although Lane didn't get his conveyors and elevators, the library stack would prove adequate for years to come, and would accommodate wandering and browsing of readers when the stacks were opened to all readers later in the century.

While Eleanor Elkins Widener was flexible on matters of library economy, she remained steadfast in her intent to memorialize her son; and as the Deed of Trust makes clear, Eleanor Elkins Widener retained extraordinary control over her gift. She named herself trustee of the funds she gave in trust, retained sole right to hire a curator of her son's collection, and gave herself permission, as Trustee, to use the funds she gave to increase her son's collection. Harvard was to become trustee only after her death, but only the family would ever be permitted to add books to the Harry Elkins Widener Collection.

In other ways her wishes, too, were firm. She held complete control over the building site. "Harvard sets apart for the location of the said building the present site of Gore Hall," states the Deed of Trust, "and gives to the donor the right, at her own expense, to demolish the same and to make use of any salvage in the erection of the new building. Harvard also give authority to the Donor to do grading and landscape work on the grounds in the immediate vicinity of the new library building to complete and set off the same, all of which work is to be done at the sole cost and expense of the Donor."

Eleanor left a large stamp indeed on her son's library. The Memorial Rooms were set apart, demarcated architecturally and programatically from the rest of the library; the Widener books were never to be mixed into the general collection or housed elsewhere. Eleanor set aside a special trust fund of $150,000 worth of securities (with herself as trustee) to hire her curator and care for the rooms and the books. As the Deed stipulates, "The Donor reserves the right to nominate and appoint the custodian or curator in charge of said Memorial Hall and memorial library, and upon her death that right shall devolve upon her oldest living child for the time being. Upon the death of the Donor's last surviving child, the right to appoint the custodian shall vest in Harvard."

This document, though quite clear in its stipulations, has been the inspiration for a minor mythology at Harvard regarding Eleanor's gift and her wishes. "[Harvard] particularly agrees that it will not permit any structures of any kind to be erected in the courts around which said building is constructed, but that the same shall be kept open for light and air; and that it will not make or permit to be made any changes, additions or alterations to the exterior of the said building or to the portions of the building hereinbefore specially set apart, to wit., Memorial Hall and the library room in the rear thereof, or in the entrance halls on first floor and main stairway to second floor." And so to this day do members of Harvard's Crimson Key Society tell visitors to campus that the building cannot be altered, although the Widener family has made practical modifications to that requirement over the years. Some guides further regale their audiences with eccentric trivia: that ice cream (Harry's favorite dessert) must be served in the dining halls; that incoming students must pass a swim test (had Harry learned to swim at Harvard, instead of collecting books, he would have survived, or so the guides assure us); that fresh flowers appear mysteriously in the Memorial Rooms. It is altogether such a delightful mythology that it seems churlish to point out that the Deed makes no mention anywhere of ice cream or swim tests. Neither does a fresh-flower mandate appear here; it would not come until 1916, when Eleanor wrote a letter to George Parker Winship, curator of the Harry Elkins Widener

Collection. Winship conveyed the request it contained to President Lowell as follows:

> My dear President Lowell;–
> Mrs. Rice has written to me as follows: -
>
> 783 PARK AVENUE March 23rd, 1916
> Dear Mr. Winship -
>
> Will you please see that at all times fresh flowers are kept on your table by the photograph of my dear son Harry, the same to be paid for out of the fund set aside for the maintenance of the Memorial Room. This is the only requeest I make, and I beg of you to see that it is always carried out. With kindest regards – I am Very sincerely, Eleanor Elkins Rice
>
> She asked me to keep this letter on file here. Will you kindly have this copy of it kept with other documents relating to her gift of the Library so that it might form so far as possible a part thereof?

And so it has been on file, now forming "a part thereof" in the University Archives. As for the flowers, they have always been ordered by the curatorial staff of the Memorial Room from local florists arriving by standard delivery at the West Door along with all other parcels, packages, and mail bound for Widener.

WHILE THE TERMS OF THE GIFT WERE STILL UNDER DISCUSSION, the faculty buzzed with talk about the new library. Few, however, mentioned either fresh flowers or the efficient movement of books in the stacks; what impressed many professors who viewed the plans was the sheer scale of the new building. Professor Barrett Wendell wrote to Lowell in October 1912:

> On looking at the elevation of the new library, I feel greatly sure that what will make it look extremely out of proportion with the other buildings is chiefly the height of columns in the front. Would it be possible to suggest that Trumbauer execute another elevation, with two stories of columns, each evidently a little less than half the height of these now contemplated? With the intervening cornice, this would much reduce the apparent height of

Widener's front in four-color lithography on a postcard (above), and a view of the new building from Massachusetts Avenue before Wigglesworth Hall was built (below).

the building, bringing it into something more nearly like accordance with its surroundings.

Lowell's response was curt and to the point: "The difficulty in your suggestion," he replied, "is that Mrs. Widener told me that she thought the elevation of the Library perfect as it is. She may change her mind, but I think it would be unwise to make any suggestions, verb. sap. [word to the wise]."

Others lamented the loss of Gore Hall. Albert Bushnell Hart, Professor of Government, wrote Lowell to bemoan the loss of Gore Hall: "Not only will a building disappear which is familiar to the eye of thousands of graduates, but with it goes the seal of Cambridge, which will be like the state of Ohio without a derelict canal boat." Hart proposed that part of the old library be saved as a memorial, even perhaps incorporated into the new library, a plan that Lowell rejected as contrary to the wishes of Mrs. Widener. Lowell respected Eleanor Widener's plans utterly, noting in a letter to another critic of the building that, when it came to the design of the library as a whole, his hands were largely tied: " . . . Mrs. Widener does not give the University the money to build a library, but has offered to build a library satisfactory in external appearance to herself."

Other serious concerns were raised about the interior plans of the library. In a letter to Coolidge dated October 28, 1912, Herbert Putnam of the Library of Congress averred that his opinion "[a]s to . . . the monumental effect of the building or its relation to the group . . . would be quite superfluous, and impertinent as against the judgment of your committee of advisors. . . ." What worried Putnam, however, was at once more quotidian and more vital to the life of the library: the rather haphazard positioning of the delivery desk, which was to be situated at one end of the stacks rather than at a more central point. Putnam had written to Lowell as well, but the president was dismissive of his concerns. "A scholar's library is a different thing from a public library, and the number of books used through the delivery room is comparatively small in proportion to those used in the stacks. My interest in the arrangement of the library is centered about making it as useful as possible for scholars who are engaged in study by providing them with working rooms, and with stalls or cubicles, leading off the stacks. The arrangement of the delivery room has seemed to me less important . . . ." While Lowell betrays here a lack of concern for standard practice, the library he envisions is innovative; it puts the massive resources of the stack close at the scholar's hand, reuniting books and readers in an intimacy that nineteenth-century design had long precluded.

Despite the formidable demands of such a massive construction project—protracted legal negotiations, disagreements between librarians and architects, and the challenge of running a library-in-exile while awaiting the construction of the new building—Widener rose in stupendously short order. Gore Hall was torn down in less than three months; by the winter of 1913, more than 500,000 volumes had been moved into temporary shelving throughout the university. In August 1913, Coolidge wrote Walter Lichtenstein, his agent in Europe, telling him that "[s]omething like fifty thousand bricks are being put into [the new library] every day." At about the same time President Lowell wrote to Mrs. Widener, assuring her that the library was "literally growing out of the ground, and it does look great in proportion, suggesting the vast services it will render to scholarship in the future." Construction went forward so quickly that librarian William Coolidge Lane lost the chance to make much-wanted changes to the design of the stack and the placement of elevators.

Throughout the construction of the new library, books chugged here and there about the Yard in Carney's two electric trucks. The life of the library went on; "the few books damaged by previous rains" that dripped through Randall's leaky roof "were taken apart, dried, ironed, and resewed by our binder." The annual shelf examination carried out in Summer 1913, found a mere 360 books mishelved, with a further two thousand on the right shelf but in the wrong position—this for nearly six hundred thousand well-travelled books.

THE NEW LIBRARY OPENED AT COMMENCEMENT, 24 JUNE 1915. The keynote speaker was Senator Henry Cabot Lodge, whose bellicose address connected the loss of Harry with the war in

Europe. "This noble gift to learning comes to us with the shadow of a great sorrow resting on it," Cabot said in opening, and expanded on the *Titanic* disaster and Harry's death with lines from Milton's *Lycidas*: "That fatal and perfidious bark / Built in th' eclipse, and rigged with curses dark / That sank so low that sacred heart of thine." The library, he noted, is "a monument to a lover of books, and in what more gracious guise than this can a man's memory go down to a remote posterity." But Widener Library is more than this, as it gives "one of the best assurances a university can have of strength and fame and numbers, for a great library draws men and women in search of education as a garden of flowers draws the bees. Carlyle indeed went even further when he said 'The true university of these days is a collection of books.' Such a library as this is not only a pillar of support to learning but it is a university in itself."

Lodge closed by recalling Whitman's verse: "Camerado, this is no book, / Who touches this book touches a man. / (Is it night? Are we here together alone?) / It is I you hold and who holds you, / I spring from these pages into your arms / decease calls me forth." Here again, Lodge contrasted the enduring properties of books with the ephemeral qualities of human life, considered especially in light of war. "Rightly considered in this aspect," he continued, "the books mean so much now, just now, when freedom of speech, and freedom of thought, when liberty and democracy are in jeopardy every hour . . . ." And finally, Lodge quoted Milton again—this time the *Aeropagitica*, his famed tract on intellectual freedom: "For books are not absolutely dead things, but do contain a potency of life in them to be as active as that soul whose progeny they are. . . . I know they are as lively, and as vigorous, as those fabulous Dragon's teeth; and being sown up and down may chance to spring up armed men." In his enthusiasm, Lodge altered the sentiment of a Milton who recognized the risk society takes in permitting freedom of the press. Milton meant that men, armed by books, may indeed spring up in usurpation—and yet the good of their freedom outweighs even this potential danger. But Lodge read the passage differently: the university's task in the coming conflict was to provide well-trained gentlemanly minds and bodies for the officer corps, and this is a task to which Harvard must dedicate its splendid new library. Where Milton had sounded a cautionary note about the perils and responsibilities of liberty, Lodge issued a cultured call to arms.

While war raged in far-off places, at Harvard all was peaceful following Commencement. Now, the books flowed into Widener from across the tranquil Yard. The first, carried by Coolidge in the ceremonial procession, was John Downame's *Christian Warfare*, the only book of John Harvard's bequest then thought to have survived to the present day. The balance of the books began arriving from Randall Hall and twelve other scattered repositories; 1,300 volumes arrived that afternoon by electric truck, packed into crates built to align with the size of the new library's shelves. More flowed in at the rate of about fifty thousand a week; some weeks, as many as seventy thousand books were delivered to the new library. The move into Widener was a bigger feat than the move out of Gore had been: in fourteen weeks, nearly seven hindred thousand books flowed into the new building, according to Carney's careful notes (he had predicted it would take twenty weeks). But they must have seemed very few in the new library, which held space enough on its shelves for one and a half million books more.

John Downame's Christian Warfare, *which in 1915 was thought to be the last surviving book of John Harvard's bequest (other candidates have been identified since) and was the first to be shelved in Widener.*

Decease Calls Me Forth

PART TWO
COLOSSUS

The cover of the June 1915 special issue of Harvard Illustrated Magazine.

WILLIAM COOLIDGE LANE HERALDED THE OPENING OF the Harry Elkins Widener Memorial Library in the pages of *Library Journal*, May 1915: "The outlook from the top of the broad steps and from the windows . . . is a delightful one," he wrote, "with the tower of Memorial Hall rising above the trees." Although memorials now dominated the view, the prospect was not a gloomy one; Memorial Hall's gothic caprice contrasted nicely, to Lane's eye, with Widener's soft classicism. "Three high portals under the colonnade," Lane continued, "give admission through doors of handsome wrought iron and glass to a vestibule, and thence through swinging doors to a dignified entrance hall thirty-six feet broad and fifty feet in length," the broad lines of which are dressed in buttery Botticino marble "beautifully but not conspicuously veined." The view, notes Lane, is "so designed that even from the very entrance one will catch a glimpse of the portrait of young Harry Widener" hung in the Memorial Room at the top of the first flight of the grand staircase.

Long before the first reader had climbed the front stairs and passed through the glass-and-iron doors to catch a glimpse of Harry's portrait, Lane's staff, and Frank Carney in particular, had been immersed in the minutiae of bringing a large building to life. In his notes on rules and procedures for work in the new library, Carney had noted that staff would enter chiefly not through the grand entrance hall, but via the more prosaic East Door on ground level. In an aside to doorkeepers, he noted that "[s]oliciters, peddlers, and such like are not allowed in the building." In his neat, backward-sloping library hand, Carney crisply rattled off more rules intended to keep life in the library orderly:

A view of the entrance hall soon after Widener opened, with the door to the Memorial Rooms and the portrait of Harry Elkins Widener visible at the top of the stairway.

> The stacks are not open to the general student body or to the public [.] Officers of the University and holders of special cards of admission are allowed to enter the stacks.
>
> Holders of cards of admission are requested to keep their cards in sight as those in charge of the stacks are required to challenge anyone using the stacks who is unknown to them.
>
> It would be well for men working regularly in the stacks to give the number of the stack cubicle where they are working … so that these can be easily found when called for, or in case they ask to have books kept longer than one day….
>
> All books left on tables will be put in their places on the shelves unless marked Reserve…[.] Books so reserved must be charged at the Delivery Desk with giving the name of the Cubicle where the books are reserved.
>
> The Stack attendants must constantly be on watch to see that unauthorized persons do not enter into the stacks[.] They are particularly cautioned to see that lights are turned off when not in use.

Here and elsewhere, Frank Carney provides tantalizing clues about the nature of the working life in Widener. He tells us, for instance, that the Head janitor earned a salary of $80 per month, while the watchman and all-important messengers received $60; "school boys" hired to page books got $40–better than the fifteen women hired as cleaners at $10 per month each (the woman in charge got $30 per month while one male cleaner, responsible for the windows and marble, received the relatively princely sum of $50 for a month's work). He sketches the switchboard for the intercom phones; accounts for vacuum cleaning apparatus, keys for study holders and others, and work on the building's system of fans, which needed frequent repair. "Keep the stacks at as low a temperature as possible," he writes, "between 60 and 68 . . . . The heat in the stalls can be regulated," he adds optimistically, "by turning on and off the individual radiators." As building superintendent, Carney's mandate extended beyond heating, cooling, and cleaning; he notes the catalogue department's need for typewriters with "library key-board[s]" featuring orthographies for "English, Armenian, Bulgarian, Greek, Polish, Russian, and Servian."

Once readers began making their way to the second-floor delivery desk and calling for books, Carney duly recorded progress in the work of bringing volumes from the far reaches of the stack. "The stack work is carried on through a central station on the fourth floor," he writes:

> When the boy returns with [a] book, the time is noted and the book brought to the slide back of the Delivery desk. In this way it is possible to keep track of the boys and state definitely whether there was delay in finding any particular book. In case the book is out, NOS is placed against the number in the record book, showing that the book was not in place when sent for. The NOS slips are reported immediately to the Delivery desk and if it is necessary to look up the book further, the slip is turned over to the shelf examiner or inspector who tries to find the misplaced book. In the first few months of the college year, owing to the unsatisfactory condition of the shelves after the moving, about one slip in twelve was returned with NOS on it. Later in the year when the shelves were examined and put in good order this percentage was reduced to one in fifty. Should a slip be received for a book in a part of the stack where a boy has just been sent—particularly in the West stack, which is farthest away from the central station—the number is telephoned across on the internal telephone. At present to make the connectionon [sic] any but the fourth floor it is necessary to call the supts. office and request the office boy to ring the proper floor.
>
> It is possible to speak from any of the phones to the central station. It seems desirable to have signal bells on each floor connected with the central station so that the boys can be called on from any part of the stack.

Although President Lowell had expected the new library to function as an open stack, it was administered as a closed stack, and those who enjoyed the right of access in the new library suffered for their privilege. Carney notes that "[s]tudents and visiting scholars (using stalls in the stacks) were obliged to furnish their own tables and chairs. This condition existed until the first of February [1916] when a start was made in furnishing the three

A view from the landing in front of the entrance to the Memorial Rooms shows light streaming through the front entrance and the windows of the Main Reading Room.

The Rotunda in the Widener Memorial Rooms.

hundred stalls in the stack with tables and chairs. By the middle of March the stalls were equipped with 250 tables and chairs and twenty high tables for temporary consultation of books."

Elsewhere, too, Carney had more than his share of troubles. When the weather turned chilly that first fall term, he found it impossible to maintain a comfortable temperature in the Reading Room. Blasts of icy wind forced their way in through the grand front entrance, bearing dust and dead leaves up the marble stairs to swirl among the students at their numbered places along the tables. The elevators, too, vexed him, "partly due to their sensitiveness and partly to the inexperience and carelessness of the staff." He further noted that the main elevator was used only for library business, as a license was required to operate it. By 1918, Carney could record that "[a]n engineer is now on the job at all times and finds plenty to do keeping the elevators in commission[.] A great many of our difficulties are caused by misuse—largely by our boys," who, he indulgently adds, are "born with mischevious traits," and to whom "the elevators offer a flourishing field

Widener's catalog and delivery rooms, with the stack entrance visible at left.

for their exploits ... naturally to the detriment of the elevator."

It was at about this time that Carney recorded the first in a string of burglary attempts in Widener, which collectively will become infamous for their fecklessness and ignominy. On the night of August 30, 1918, he reported, "[t]he night watchman heard the noise [sic] crash of glass and started about the building to discover the cause of the noise. His walking with a lighted lantern probably frightened the burglar away and it is doubtful if they he [sic] ever got inside the building. We were unable to discover that anything was missing and cannot concern [sic] what the thief was after."

But for Carney, none of these challenges—neither crime, nor arctic winds, nor broken-down elevators—loomed larger, ultimately, than that of the bathrooms. "The need of better toilet facilities has been pressed upon us during the past year by several rather distressing experiences," Carney noted in his customarily dry tone in 1918. "At present everyone using the stack is obliged to go to the basement to reach the public toilet. This in

Colossus 59

the case of a man using one of the top floors of the stack is a particularly long trip consuming a considerable amount of time. . . . An emergency toilet for the use of the staff on the Reading Room floor would be a desirable thing. This toilet," he pleads, "could be kept locked with a limited outside use on request. . . ." Finally, the toilets got the better even of the unflappable Carney, who threw up his hands and simply declared that "[I]t was a mistake in planning the building not to provide more toilets." To Carney, the problem of the university library was not a question of its role as laboratory, but as lavatory.

Carney also notes one of the first impacts the distant war had on the library. "In the Memorial rooms and in the corridor at the main entrance the badly matched marble was replaced by the marble contractors. They claimed that oweing [sic] to the war it was difficult to procure the right kind of marble to finish the job." This would hardly be the last tremor of the Great War in Widener or in the university at large.

IN HIS MAGISTERIAL *THREE CENTURIES OF HARVARD*, SAMUEL Eliot Morison wrote that "[a]s early as 1915 one can snuff the approach of war in President Lowell's reports." It was an odor caught earlier at Harvard than elsewhere, he notes:

> At the western university where I was teaching when the war broke out in Europe, it seemed to the average student as unreal as the Wars of the Roses; returning to Harvard early in 1915, one was on the outskirts of battle. The first ambulance and hospital units had gone over from the Harvard Medical and Dental Schools; scores of young graduates were enlisting in the Canadian and the British expeditionary forces, the Foreign Legion, and the Lafayette flying squadron; sympathy for the allied cause was unconcealed; not for a moment was the Harvard community neutral in thought or deed. . . . The "Manifesto of the German Intellectuals" and the destruction of the University of Louvain threw American opinion definitely on the side of the Allies; and Harvard called two of Louvain's exiled professors to her faculty early in 1915.

Thorstein Veblen, too, noted the effect of the war on American academia, forecasting that the Great War would thrust it into a leadership role in the world's intellectual culture. As with Morison, he argued that German intellectuals had squandered their leading role in service to the militantly nationalistic enterprise of German domination in Europe—a stance that each European country's intelligentsia had more or less taken as the continent had gone about the business of turning itself into a powder keg. The coming end of European intellectual prominence "promise[d] to leave the American men of learning in a strategic position, in the position of a strategic reserve," who would need to take up the work of sheltering learned culture from "the one-eyed forces of reaction and partisanship" threatening to overtake the world. Veblen's analysis might have less described the current war than prophesied the next one; nonetheless, he had caught a general current of opinion among American academics, who believed they would help to lead the world out of the darkness of war. And Archibald Cary Coolidge, Harvard's worldly library director, made sure that Widener would join the effort. "The Harvard University Library, like the one at Yale, is collecting data on the European war," *Library Journal* announced in 1915. "Books, of which there are already more than a few, war maps, files of newspapers from the war zone and from neutral countries, official despatches, and other like material are included in the collection, which is already at the service of students."

For all its grandeur and ostentation, Widener was an artifact of a simpler time in American higher education. Its vast marble spaces were meant not merely to memorialize one man, but also to ratify the almost liturgical role played by the college in the life of America's elite. Despite the turn toward research and professional education pioneered by Eliot at Harvard, as well as at such other institutions as Johns Hopkins and the University of Chicago, college life had become an important part of the political economy of the Gilded Age—of that riot of urges and ostentations Veblen had famously described as "conspicuous consumption." Yet Widener quickly proved itself not only a conspicuous building, but an adaptable institution as well. Its great capacity for the storage of books, combined with its profusion of working

Widener's cannon, seemingly pointed at the spire of the future Memorial Church.

space and its central location, rendered it uniquely qualified to help put Harvard on a war footing. In both this war and the next, Widener would offer its spaces for the use of civilian relief work and war-related research projects.

At war's end, young men who had cut short their educations to serve overseas streamed back into the Yard. It took some time, however, for Harvard to become demilitarized. Military education continued at Harvard, the department of Military Science complementing the curriculum with such courses as "Motorized Traction" and "Gunnery." On 23 September 1919, the *Crimson* reported, "[a] large 155 mm. G.P.F. rifle . . . was put into firing position by the men of the regular army detachment on duty at Harvard and now rests 'in battery' in front of the Widener Library." Firing a ninety-five pound shell with a maximum range of some ten miles, the cannon was "one of a type and calibre that proved themselves very efficient in the recent war. . . . and is remarkably accurate." Suddenly, the nation's greatest academic library was also the best-armed.

But Widener did not keep its armament for long. Other

wartime changes, however, proved more durable. Although dedicated to the memory of one man, Widener's memorial function expanded dramatically in the years during and following the war. Eleanor Elkins Widener had originally stipulated that no further memorials would be permitted within her library, but the war had softened her feelings on the matter. Too many Harvard men died in the conflict to ignore their loss—and further, it seems, Eleanor came to connect Harry's death with their sacrifice. To Eleanor and many American elites, the loss of such men as Harry on the *Titanic* had exempified the ideals of duty and honor that the upper classes held dear, and prefigured their contribution to the war effort.

For a time, then, memorials proliferated in Widener. William Coolidge Lane, himself president of the Memorial Society, oversaw ceremonial functions in the library and beyond its walls, and for a time, Widener was home to a parade of wreaths and tributes. The most significant tribute, however, would come at the instance of President Lowell, who in 1921 commissioned John Singer Sargent to paint a diptych of murals to

Top: Sargent's Gassed. Above: *Studies for the Widener murals.* Overleaf: *Sargent's murals,* Death and Victory *(left) and* Coming of the Americans *(right), which bracket the door to the Memorial Rooms.*

Colossus 63

HAPPY THOSE WHO WITH A GLOWING FAITH
IN ONE EMBRACE CLASPED DEATH AND VICTORY

THEY CROSSED THE SEA CRUSADERS KEEN TO HELP
THE NATIONS BATTLING IN A RIGHTEOUS CAUSE

commemorate Harvard war dead. Sargent (who complained, on his first visit to the front, about the lack of grandeur in the blasted scenery) had already made paintings of the war, including the searing *Gassed*–a massive canvas depicting a line of blinded soldiers making their way across a blasted, muddy field while the tragic panoply of the war, from off-duty soldiers' soccer games to aerial bombardment, fills the background. Since the end of the conflict, Sargent had been pursuing public art; at the time of the Widener commission he was working on his series of murals in Boston's Museum of Fine Arts. The two images Sargent devised to hang on either side of the entrance to the Memorial Rooms depict, on the left, the apotheosis of a solider killed in battle (entitled *Death and Victory*) and, on the right, soldiers marching to the aid of the beleagured nations of Western Europe (*Coming of the Americans*). Drawing on such popular sources as war bond posters, newspaper supplements, and the advertising imagery, Sargent depicted his soldiers as bright, energetic, idealized Harvard men. While many critics interpreted Sargent's murals as little more than glorified propaganda posters, Lowell used Sargent to pursue a more complex symbolic agenda, casting the war effort as a crusade, and Harvard's dead as religious sacrifice. But to Lowell, even the evident patriotism of the murals was insufficient. He had supported the war ardently, supported also Woodrow Wilson's League of Nations (which the bellicose Henry Cabot Lodge, who had delivered the address on Widener's opening, most famously opposed). With Sargent, he composed a pair of verses to be inscribed beneath the murals which, together, sum up Lowell's feelings about the war: "They crossed the sea crusaders keen to help / The nations battling in an enlightened cause"; and "Happy those, who with that glowing faith / In one embrace clasped Death and Victory."

Sargent's murals were given a mixed reception, and remained controversial for a generation. Student groups who proffered sympathy for Germany and, closer to World War Two, neutrality for the United States, regularly protested the presence of the images in Widener. But the paintings, which solemnize the soldiers' sacrifice and cast it in world-historical terms, achieve an effect different from the simplistic jingoism of the wartime posters from which their imagery is drawn. At the same time they efface the irony and frankness of so much of the great art to come out of the war–not only Sargent's own depiction of the conflict in *Gassed*, but that of war poets like Wilfred Owen, whose "Dulce et decorum est" repudiates the cleanly, heroic notion of death offered in Sargent's mural. The soldier in Sargent's *Death and Victory* may be a victim of poison gas–peaceable, tinged with the divine, his image is vastly different from the one offered by Owen, with "white eyes writhing" in a face "like a devil's sick of sin," with blood that "Come[s] gargling from the froth-corrupted lungs, / Obscene as cancer, bitter as the cud / Of vile, incurable sores on innocent tongues…." Sargent, by contrast, depicts precisely the kind of "old lie" Owen complains is offered to children who thrill to war: *"Dulce et decorum est pro patria mori."*

And yet, perhaps the sweetest and most decorous tribute to Harvard war dead had come to Widener before America actually entered the war. Henry Weston Farnsworth graduated in the year of Harry Elkins Widener's death; three years later, he was killed in action in the battle for the Fortin Navarin in Champagne while serving in the French Foreign Legion. Henry had a bookish bent, though unlike Harry Elkins Widener he was no antiquarian. He liked not to collect, but to read; his favorite authors included Ibsen and Tolstoy. He seemed to have writerly ambitions as well–immediately after graduation he had made his way to the Balkans in hopes of writing about the troubles there; he joined the Foreign Legion in order to gather material for a book or an article about the growing conflict in Europe. But by the time he saw his first action, he was thoroughly caught up in the spirit of the war. He was impressed both by Gallic mettle and by the wildly cosmopolitan flavor of life in the Legion, where the melismatic songs of Hellenic Turkish volunteers mixed with the Tongan war chants of soldiers from Fiji. After his death, Henry's parents endowed a room in Widener "for the leisurely reading of such standard books as Henry Farnsworth loved." Attractively furnished with comfortable chairs and filled with a simply organized collection of general interest books, the Farnsworth Room

helped to domesticate Widener's austere and forbidding interior. The gift was brilliant—it answered a deep need among undergraduates hungry for the simple joy of reading and reflected poignantly the youthful, careless bonhomie with which Henry Farnsworth, like so many of his classmates, went to war. The Farnsworths created an axis of commemoration in Widener, with two opposed, albeit not exclusive, poles. On the one hand there was the memory of Harry, the consummate connoisseur, whose chambers of pale marble and dark wood were at once intimate and forbidding, and whose conspicuously valuable books represented the apogee of a young man's transformation into a gentleman and bibliophile; on the other hand Henry, who died in uniform, and whose memorial room was meant as a tranquil, casual sanctuary in the midst of a busy, ordered, and exclusive library.

Top: *Bookplate for volumes in the Farnsworth Room Collection.* Above: *A postcard view of the Farnsworth Room.*

The first curator of the Farnsworth Room, Florence Milner, brimmed over with zeal. Her workaday journal of life in the Farnsworth Room is filled with ardent expressions of the power of books—the literary kind found in the room—to remake the lives of dissolute students. "When they [students] finally take a book from the shelves," she wrote in her first entry, "and settle into the most comfortable place available at the time, then they have come into their own." Throughout her journal, she records ever more purple versions of the literary epiphany her room thrusts on even the most backwards youth. "One young man," she writes, "whose life had evidently been cramped and barren, failed to remove his hat. He walked slowly toward the shelves and gazed about. By degrees the expression of his face changed—his was a slow moving mind—and then his hat came off. He had heard the voice of the room." Milner returns often to this image: a shabby youth, a scrappy arriviste who landed a spot at Harvard through merit and mettle, who now, basking in the genteel atmosphere of the Farnsworth Room, discovers his will to culture. In this respect, she prefigures the meritocratic ideals of the Harvard of James Bryant Conant, still two decades away.

It is hard, however, to imagine that if the adventuresome Henry Farnsworth were to speak from beyond the grave, he would use such an opportunity to give a lesson on manners. Yet to Florence Milner, Henry's room was meant not to inspire or inflame but to refine, to anneal, to ripen the civilization that lay dormant in the Harvard man's soul. The pleasurable trance of literature was a tonic—and yet it was important to her that the whole room, and not merely the choice of books on its shelves, ennoble and uplift.

Henry's mother, Lucy, found a kindred spirit in Florence Milner. On January 12, 1917, she wrote her curator a warm letter:

> Every word of your letter is of intense interest to us—We have copied it to send to all our daughters—We are more grateful to you than I can express for letting us share in this way with your hours in Henry's room & letting us see with your eyes the boys who use it—
>
> I agree with you the reading habit is everything—let them read only novels for a year, and all the rest will follow....

> It makes us very happy that one who understands &
> empathizes as you do is the presiding genius of the room.

And this "presiding genius," moreover, helped to make the room popular. Milner's attendance figures for the first year show that the room was a busy place; at its height in November 1917 it hosted 3,667 visitors, and even in its lowest month (excepting the summer months between terms) the room saw more than 1,800 students pass through the door. Milner's success was surely due in part to her enthusiuasm for the mission of the room; no doubt it also relied on her moderating influence in a building designed to communicate power, privilege, and rigor to the students who used it. Milner's discipline was of a subtler sort than her male colleagues with their imprecations of honor, their suspensions of privileges, and their visits with the Dean. On March 15, 1917, she discovers a young man dog-earing a page in a book. "He very amiably recognized my implied rebuke," she writes, "when I gave him a slip of paper and asked him to use it as a bookmark and so avoid marring our handsome books." Such rebuke was both softened and enhanced by the comfortable environs of the room itself, which Milner took pains to decorate with flowers of a variety called "Honesty," which she collected from the Farnsworth family's Dedham gardens. In a sense, Milner domesticated the library—she supplied within its marble interior a soft, almost maternal retreat.

Milner saw self-cultivation as part of her charge. To bring Harvard's rowdies into a state of perpetual learning, she must herself continue to grow and ripen in genteel spirit. Reshelving Henry James, she dedicated herself to reading his entire œuvre, so as better to share his gifts with readers. Not long after solemnizing this quest in her journal, she transcribes a passage from James's "The Great Good Place":

> The library was a benediction—high and clear and plain . . . but with something in its arched amplitude unconfused and brave and gay. He should never forget, he knew, the throb of immediate perception with which he first stood there, a single glance around sufficing to show him that it would give him what for years he had desired. He had not had detachment, but there was

Above: *Arnold B. Cranston was one of Florence Milner's student assistants when he sketched this scene in the Farnsworth Room's log book.*

> detachment here...the sense of a great silver bowl from which he could ladle up all the melted hours. He strolled about . . . recognizing from shelf to shelf every dear old book that he had had to put off or never returned to; every deep distinct voice of another time that in the hubbub of the world he had had to take for unlost or unheard.

As we have seen before, libraries, for James, are places suffused with longing. Of this Jamesian condition of suppressed release, Milner notes that "the Farnsworth Room echoes it somewhat."

BEYOND THE COMFORTING CONFINES OF THE FARNSWORTH Room and the marble stairway with Sargent's commanding murals, other Widener spaces made history in their own, more practical ways. In May 1915, the *Library Journal* discussed the library's role in the changing complexion of the American university, noting that Widener Library "has the central and commanding position in the famous Yard, and indeed the splendor of its famous façade dwarfs the historic brick buildings of this most ancient of our colleges." And yet what catches the attention of the *Journal* is "not so much the spacious and lofty reading room as . . . the several hundred study rooms, cubicle-like, which surround the stack, giving special facilities for the individual work of professors and students."

True to professor Emerton's hopes, Widener offered ample room for scholarly work, and critics both within the Harvard community and beyond the Yard agreed that the studies and cubicles included in the Widener stacks were the new library's most innovative feature. In comparison to Gore Hall, of course, the vistas of work space were dizzying. And yet even such a generous apportionment quickly began to seem too small—for the demand was high, not only from students and faculty, but from all quarters of the community. Petitions for studies had begun to arrive in September 1912—almost as soon as plans were publicly available.

Archibald Cary Coolidge's expectations for study holders were exacting, as he articulated in rules laid down as early as 1912. "The assignment of studies to professors will be for one year," Coolidge ruled, "and in the question of reassignment, the extent of the use made of the room will be taken into account. It is

Widener's stack, book-free and gleaming.

expected that ordi[na]rily a professor will be able to continue in the same study from year to year, but he will not have a right to retain it during a leave of absence or after his return to count on having the same one as before." The library would strive to offer use of studies to as many scholars as possible, temporarily reassigning the room of scholars who went out of town for the summer or on sabbatical.

The indefatigable Coolidge seems to have fielded and managed study requests himself through the first years of the library. There are letters in which he urges professors to share their precious studies with less-fortunate colleagues or to move into other quarters to accommodate other uses. One letter, addressed to Coolidge and requesting assignment, complains about the talking and shouting of "attendants" in the stacks. Coolidge's answer, 29 March 1918: "The boys in the stack are undoubtedly noisy. The difficulty about restraining them is that the men who had charge of such things have been taken from us by the draft and are irreplaceable."

That same day Coolidge writes to C. H. Grandgent, "The pressure on me for studies is getting considerable. I have just had a plaintive appeal from Mercier asking for a place to work. Neither you nor Sheldon make frequent use of Room 117. I should like therefore, unless there is some good reason to the contrary, to put Mercier in with you." Grandgent and Sheldon agree, and for a time three scholars shared the single cramped study.

17 January 1917, Coolidge to A.H. Herrick:

> The situation about the rooms is this. The demand considerably exceeds the supply. The rooms are not all fully used, but you will understand that I can not go to a professor and tell him that I think he is not making use of his space and had better give it up. I have tried in some cases hinting to people that if they did not need their quarters there were others who could make good use of them. These hints have usually met with conspicuously little success.

For all their obvious value, the high demand among faculty for studies troubled Coolidge nearly as much as queues at the toilets vexed Frank Carney; nor were faculty members the only competitors for working space in the new library. Amidst his papers are letters from faculty requesting phone lines for their studies, which Coolidge's policy forbade. He deals carefully and yet sternly, too, with departments who do not seem to make use of the space they have requested, reflecting pressures on him to meet researchers' needs. The request of the Harvard University Press indicates that demand for space in the stacks existed outside the faculty: a letter from C. Chester Lane states that the Syndics of the Harvard University Press (as the editorial board of the Press then styled itself) wish to be able to use "a workroom where the examples of fine printing now in the Library might be readily examined," as well as meeting space for the board. A list compiled in 1915 records requests for rooms from the following groups: the Cambridge Historical Society, the International Polity Federation, and the Numismatic Collection; the Warren House Sanskrit Library ("1 room with diffused light allowing for growth"–though growth of what the list refuses to say); the Western Historical Collection ("Room for display"); the Graduate School of Business Administration ("1 large room near general collection of Business School Books" and "1 small conference room (or 2) Increase of stack facilities / Storage space in basement / with stacks"); the Department of Classics (large study, including "table & elbow room for 20 men" as well as "1 smaller for seminary work, all "adjoining each other and near all necessary books") and the Department of Economics (1 large seminary room—to accommodate "chairs for 60 men"—as well as 1 large or two fair-sized offices and a smaller seminary room for meeting 25 or thirty advanced students at a time); 1 room each for Education, English, French, German, and Government; the Division of Mathematics (1 room for dept. library "providing liberally for future growth and students who wish to work there"); 1 room for the Bureau of Municipal Research, one study for Physics, and 2 rooms on the top floor for Drama.

Ephraim Emerton was duly thrilled to see his call for study space, voiced as early as 1899, finally fulfilled, and so generously; the encroachment on that space for uses other than research and reflection, however, already had begun, and would not be remedied until the completion of the latest renovation of the stacks in the twenty-first century.

AS PROFESSORS—AND OTHERS—WENT TO WORK IN THE STACK, Frank Carney's shelving staff were busy filling it with Harvard's growing collection. The still-empty basement, meanwhile, was turned over to the American Library Association's War Service as a shipping center for books donated for the use of servicemen overseas. "The ebb and flow of books through the East door has kept the basement floor in a constant turmoil," Carney noted in his 1918 Building Report. "In one month over one hundred thousand volumes were shipped." After the war, Lane would bill A.L.A. for damage done to Widener's main elevator, which nearly gave out under the weight of war-service books—though Carney's report makes clear that the A.L.A. were not the only ones to blame. "An engineer is now on the job at all times and finds plenty to do keeping the elevators in commission [.] A great many of our difficulties are caused by misuse—largely by our boys. Boys seem [to] be born with mischevious traits and the elevators offer a flourishing field for their exploits[.] They are constantly playing tricks on one another while using the elevators naturally to the detriment of the elevator."

The war took its toll in other ways as well. "The last man I had to depend upon to do my personal work in my absence has been drafted," Carney complained, "making the fourth man this dept has given to the service. . . . A change will probably have to be made to woman labor but even this will have to be paid highly for in view of the increasing man power needed to win the war." As the war depleted the labor pool, Carney found himself not only relying increasingly on the labor of women; he was forced to pay them higher wages, too. "An increase in wages from fifteen to twenty cents was made to the woman cleaners. An investigation showed that our rates were lower than those paid in the public buildings about Boston. Recent agitation by this class of workers may result in legislation which will oblige us to still further increase the wages of these women. I had three or four visits from an agent of the minimum wage commission making inquiries as

The "Mass Ave Corridor" on Widener's ground level with its tiled Catalan vaults by Rafael Guastavino, Jr.

to the amount paid by us to women cleaners . . . ." It's interesting that despite the decreased manpower and the attention of students to the war effort, statistics through the war show steady increases in the number of books "chased" by pages, and in numbers of books used in studies and cubicles as well, despite a wartime decrease in the number of recorded visitors to the library from the previous year. Many Harvard students were carried off by the service—and yet those who remained were finding their way to the burgeoning number of books housed in Widener.

In the lives of students, however, the expectations of the old college came up against the possibilities of the new university. Professors expected their students to make greater use of the library's abundant resources—and yet their access to those books was carefully controlled. Widener's capacious new reading rooms were designed to dole out books placed on reserve and to handle readers' need for books pulled from the general stacks as well—books that college students could not browse directly, as the stacks were closed to them. The reading rooms quickly filled with students whose need for books—and for instruction and supervision—frequently overwhelmed staff.

Of course, problem patrons were nothing new to librarians at Harvard or elsewhere; even in Gore Hall, staff had sent out cards to readers holding missing or late books. A Gore Hall librarian must have read with shock one such card, received from a Shawmut Avenue address in Boston in the spring of 1896:

> I received your postal card this morning, relating to the map of Scotland which I received on March 16th. It was an old one (1803 or thereabouts), and I was under the impression that I might keep it. It served my purpose fairly well on the day when I got it, but has since been destroyed.
>
> Yours truly, T. Allison.

The librarian wrote back in what must have been unpleasant tones, for a disbelieving Allison wrote him again a few days later:

> Your letter of 21st. inst. caused me considerable surprise, because I am altogether unconscious of having meant any dis-

> courtesy, and now hasten to remove all misapprehension you seem to be under regarding my conduct.
>
> I was very much obliged to the young gentleman who put himself to such trouble on the 16th of March in order to procure me the map; and would certainly have had the ordinary politeness to return it at an early opportunity, had I not understood from him that I might keep it. At this distant date, I cannot recall the exact words he used (or I may possibly have misunderstood him, as I was somewhat flurried at the time); but I should certainly never have destroyed the map, had some such impression not been once conveyed to my mind.
>
> May I be allowed to say that no person who knows me whould ever have ventured to make such an imputation as your letter conveys.
>
> However, it is doubtless all due to a misunderstanding, and I am prepared to do whatever you think honourable under the circumstances. I only wish to set my conduct in its proper light.
>
> Yours truly, T. Allison.
>
> P.S.– will you kindly let the matter rest for a day or two, as I leave Boston to-morrow, not to return till beginning of week.

Allison's destruction of the map was an egregious offense; it was also unique in its time. Of the letters contained in Lane's discipline files, it is one of the few dating from the Gore Hall era. There are dozens of letters, however, from the nineteen-twenties and thirties. What was it about the new Widener Library that prompted young men to behave in a manner that would prompt one staffer to fire off the following memo to Lane in 1926:

> The enclosed list contains the names of the chief offenders in the Lower Reading Room. Every man on the list has been requested to be quiet while in the room and has failed repeatedly to comply with the request.

> I have been complemented by Professor Roger Merriman and by his instructors and assistants on the manner in which I have conducted the L.R.R. The one source of trouble which I have signally failed in ovecoming is the commuters' discussion groups of which the lists presents the chief offenders. These men regard me as more or less of a disturber of their right to talk and prevent others from studying, and do not disguise their doubts as to my authority in asking them to be quiet or to leave the room.
>
> If these men are led to understand that it is for the benefit of the fellow students and not for any satisfaction I obtain from exercising such petty authority that they are asked to refrain from conferring on mathematics, French, German, or any study while in the L.R.R., the room will be at all times the ideal place for study which it is now when they are absent. The method of bringing them to this better understanding of their obligations I leave to your better judgment. Perhaps I am wrong in suggesting that they be suspended for a time. But something should be done if the L.R.R. is to be a success.

Maintaining order in the ground floor's secluded Lower Reading Room, where books were kept on reserve for classes in Economics, Law, and Political Science, was a constant problem. At the bottom of a December 1927 letter expelling a student from the Lower Reading Room for talking and arguing with the attendant, the following note appears: "Readmitted Jan 9 / Thinks he can get along without argument but is not convinced that he was a nuisance."

Widener's troubles were well known; on 10 December 1924 an article in *The Harvard Crimson* entitled "Number of Missing Books Nears Record" told the story. "With more than 80 books already missing from the reserved shelves in the Library," it began, "this year bids fair to equal last year's record of 350 stolen books."

> In the courses in Economics, Social Ethics, and Philosophy alone, 25 books have been missing since October 1. "But the worst part of it all", complained Librarian C. A. Mahady, when interviewed across the desk of the main reading room, yesterday "is that often a single volume of a series is stolen, and then the library usually has to buy an entire new set in order to replace just one volume. Recently, several volumes of

Emerson's journals and one of the International Encyclopedia have been pilfered, and it will probably cost the library close to a hundred dollars to replace them."

Not only have books been pilfered from the main reading room, but there have been many cases of mutilation which have reduced materially the value of the books. One thoughtless student, evidently to make his labors in the stacks more comfortable, propped himself up with a big volume, with the result that the back of the book, a valuable reprint of an old Spanish edition, was completely crushed. There have also been several cases of cutting out pictures from books or magazines, some of which will be hard to replace. In fact the situation towards the end of last year had grown so bad that this year the library authorities decided to transfer some magazines such as the "Graphic" and "L' Illustration", from the periodical room to the regular stacks.

"Last year" said Mr. Mahady, "there was a regular epidemic

The studious throng in a brimful Widener Reading Room circa 1927.

of cases in which a man signed a false name in borrowing a book, with the expectation of being relieved altogether from the necessity of returning it. This year there have been no such cases."

"It is surprising," concluded Mr. Mahady, "how men will try the same trick over and over again and hope to get away with it. Why, we had one fellow who tried to slip in two applications for the same book. He was caught and reprimanded by my assistant, but, nothing daunted he tried the same trick again four hours afterwards with me.

"There is another thing, that students don't seem to understand, and that is the returning of books by 9 o'clock in the morning. Students don't realize that often there is only one copy of the book they have taken out, and that it is very much in need in the Library. Therefore they feel offended when a notice, asking them to return the book, is sent to them. We had a man last year, who kept a book so long that we had to send a messenger to get the book in his room. Later, when fined 50 cents for the service, he replied with a very sarcastic letter, in which he enclosed a dollar, which was "to be given to any student too poor to pay such an unjust fine."

But Widener's troubles involved more than a few sarcastic and unruly students. Something about the reserves system simply did not work. On the other hand, late or misplaced reserve books were hardly the only problem the library faced; the defacing of books was taken quite seriously, as shown by this letter to S. H. Askowith, May 17, 1920:

I am sorry to have my attention drawn to a volume of Murray's "Odyssey" in the Farnsworth Room, badly defaced in ink by you. This is an abuse of the privileges of that room which cannot be overlooked, and I regret to have to exclude you from all use of the Farnsworth Room for the remainder of this year. The cost of replacing the volume which you have defaced is three dollars, and I enclose a bill therefor. Please pay it promptly. The injured book you may have when it is paid for, and when we have taken the Library bookplate from it.

I must also have your assurance that you will refrain from annotating or defacing books in any part of the Library. Some such misuse of books occurs from time to time, but when it can be traced to an individual, it has to be severely dealt with under the Library rules.

Far from alone in their administration of the college's *in loco parentis* mission, librarians were part of a disciplinary regime that included faculty and administrators. Thus, discipline was meted out not only by library staff under the aegis of the librarian, but also by senior administrators at librarian's appeal. Lane frequently sought the support and intervention of his administrative superiors, as in this letter to Dean Greenough:

> I send you these three slips bearing fictitious names, along with a letter from Professor C.I. Lewis, to whom I submitted them. I am afraid there is nothing more we can do. Slips A and B, to my mind, are pretty surely written by the same hand; C might possibly be. I suspect there is nothing further we can do, but to watch out in the Reading Room.

The dean responded to Lane immediately:

> I am sorry to learn from your letter of December 8th that men continue to sign fictitious names in the Library. I agree with you that the evidence does not seem conclusive in this case. I think we may have to consider very seriously the idea of putting in the same system that would be used at a bank to verify signatures. I hope not, for it would delay the service and injure the tone of the Library, but the present situation seems to me very serious.

When librarians communicated directly with students about their infractions, they adopted the pose of their colleagues in faculty and administration, speaking of library rules in language that underscored such values as fairness, duty, and honor, as in this 1924 letter from Lane to one W. B. Pecsok:

> I regret to learn that on Tuesday evening you attempted to take an unfair advantage of others in the use of a reserved book, by filing another application for the book even while using it—and this in spite of the fact that you were warned earlier in the day that this was not permitted. It is not permitted simply because it gives one man an unfair—that is a greater—claim on a book than his fellow. When there are not enough copies of a book for everyone to have the use of a

> copy at once, everyone must be given his equal chance. It should not be difficult to see that filing duplicate applications in succession is just one of the "unfair practices and underhand methods of getting an advantage over others" that readers are publicly warned against by printed notice in the Reading Room.
>
> For the present I must exclude you from all further use of the Reading Room. If on or after Dec. 15 you can entirely satisfy me that you will faithfully observe the rules of the Room in this and other respects, I shall be happy to readmit you to its use.

Other admonishments strike the same note: in a letter regarding a student having a reserve book beyond its normal time, and not making himself available to staff at his announced desk, Lane lectured: "The few rules we have are designed simply to secure a fair and equal use among readers of what is in many respects an inadequate supply of books. You have been in the University long enough to realize that anyone who is unwilling to use the Library books with due regard for the rights of others must be excluded from their use altogether. Just as far as possible we shall carry out this principle and we expect thee cooperation of all fair-minded men in doing so."

Taken together, the efforts of librarians and their colleagues elsewhere in the university were closely coordinated. Lane wrote to Dean Greenough about another case in March 1923:

> I think I ought to report to you another case possibly calling for discipline. Elisah [sic] Canning Jr. of the Freshman class cut out one of the portraits from the 1913 Class Album. Mr. Briggs noticed the trouble after Canning had been using the book and called him in. He confessed penitently and is impressed, I think, with the wrongfulness of the act and surprised at his having yielded to the temptation to do it.

A week later, Asst. Dean David Little replied on Greenough's behalf: "I think as you suggest he is fully impressed with the wrongfulness of his act. I don't think we will have any more trouble with him. He seems to be a decent sort of fellow, . . ."

Lane took his role as an educator and mentor of the wayward

elite quite seriously; his 26 January 1921 letter to student Horatio Colony is practically a manifesto:

> I have the report from the Reading Room that you took out two volumes from the reserved books . . . and were found returning them . . . to a part of the Reading Room to which they did not belong. When confronted with the facts, you excused yourself on the ground that other men do the same, that you had no intention of stealing the books, and so it did not matter. This brings up a clear-cut issue. We who are trying to carry on the Library in the interest primarily of the readers who depend upon it, know of course that these things are done to a certain extent, but it is only now and then that we can spot the individuals and bring it home to them. Men like yourself, who take this attitude toward the Library, are the greatest difficulty we have to contend with—men who exploit the Library for their own purposes and do not play fair with their fellow students. We know the titles at this moment of other books which men are deprived of because individuals have taken them for their exclusive use. Doubtless they will return them when they get ready—unless they forget to do so. In the meantime others suffer.
>
> In each case one man is keeping from others what they have an equal right to with himself, and is so far defeating the purpose for which the Library is run.
>
> What is the remedy? The obvious thing is to deprive you, or anyone like you, of the use of that which you are unwilling to share fairly with others. That is what I have usually done in similar cases, but always with regret, for I know that such action deprives you of just what the Library wants to give you. But if such action would bring the matter home to others in such a way as to prevent their doing the same, I should feel it might be worth while to sacrifice your interests so far. But I should like to find some other way of strengthening public opinion against all practices which tend to defeat the free and fair use of the Library's resources.
>
> Your particular case is not an extreme one, but it is typical of much that goes on—largely through thoughtlessness—in all college libraries. Rather than find a penalty that "fits the crime" I should like to find a remedy for the condition. I should be glad of suggestions from you and from others.

Student Council president Henry Faxon read this letter; he expressed his own fealty to collegiate values by recommending its immediate publication in the *Crimson*.

And yet there were other rules of conduct, which covered more than talking and the use of books, as indicated in a 1923 note to Lane from C. C. Eaton, who administered the Business School Library on Widener's third floor:

My dear Mr. Lane,

> Thank you for letting me know your determination of the facts of the incident of Miss Alexander's intrusion in the reading room. I am naturally very sorry that it happened but I think now it is well understood that the ladies are requested not to enter the big reading room. I feel sure that we shall have no further instance of the sort you mention.

Further reading in Lane's correspondence with Eaton makes clear the nature of the problem: Miss Alexander, who worked for the Business School library on Widener's Third Floor, had entered the main Reading Room to find someone she had been sent to fetch—rather defiantly, we must presume, given the proscription against the admittance of women to the reading room. Even Radcliffe students weren't invited to use the reading room, for fear their presence would distract the studious Harvard men (though if the letters in Lane's files are any indication, they needed no help in distracting themselves). The reading room attendant had complained in a memo to Lane that learning had suffered a terrible blow that day, as all the young eyes in the great room had left their respective books to follow Miss Alexander as she marched down the center aisle. Women were not to use the reading room for study, even if they were students; they were sequestered in the "Radcliffe Reading Room" beyond the card catalog room next to the delivery desk—a tiny space, hardly larger than a janitorial closet.

Gender and class were precisely graded, if subtly shaded, factors of life at Harvard (and everywhere else, of course) in the early twentieth century. Harvard men were graded not only on their academic prowess, but perhaps more importantly on their gentlemanly behavior: honor, self-restraint, duty to class and country. Those who fell outside the parameters of the gentleman—women, staff and laborers, and others—were relegated to secondary, and often invisible, status. Men and women on the staff had separate space for lavatories, lockers and, at first, for lunchrooms as well. And there was a further division—the entirely invisible charwomen, janitorial workers who did the most menial cleanup labor, were relegated to separate lavatories and off-duty space of their own.

Lane's discipline files offer a vantage on the world of Widener strikingly different from Carney's attention to ventilation, elevator repair, and the payment of staff—different, but no less telling. Harvard College students were still primarily the sons of the elite; they attended college not so much to further their intellectual as their moral development, to prepare them for leadership, sacrifice, and service. That was the mission, at least, seen from the librarian's and the dean's offices. Harvard, like most colleges of that time, failed in this explicit mission—the students were as rowdy and amoral, on balance, as at any point in the history of higher education in America—but this doesn't detract from the centrality of that mission in the professional identity of the men who meted out punishment and administered advice. While most discipline problems in the library centered on the use, misuse, and abuse of books and the privilege of using them, it wasn't books as such that Lane and his colleagues were concerned about. The library staff had a role to play in the transmission of a way of life, in the inculcation of a set of values—duty, honor, sacrifice— all of which were symbolized in the portrait of Harry looking down upon the marble hall. And if these letters are any indication, it was a role that librarians at Harvard took quite seriously.

BUT AS HEADLINES IN 1931 WOULD MAKE CLEAR, WIDENER'S biggest problems with discpline and security came from without. On October 17, 1931, the *Boston Post* ran the following headline:

HARVARD BOOK THEFTS SOLVED

1804 Volumes Stolen From Widener Library Found in Dedham Home of Joel C. Williams—Graduate of College and Holder of Two Degrees Is Arrested

Claims He Purchased Books—Apprehended When Trying to Sell Them in Harvard Sq.

The subsequent article told the story of Joel Clifton Williams, a sometime schoolteacher, aspiring scholar, and holder of a graduate degree from Harvard, who had used his alumni status and amiable relations with staff to gain access to Widener's stack in order to claim nearly two thousand books as his own. The *Post*, like other newspapers, would make much of this "highly respected lifelong resident of Dedham," an "absent-minded professor." "He told police that he was a book-lover," the *Post* reported, describing the scene at his "unpretentious" home:

> In order to spare the Harvard graduate's feelings, Inspectors Carroll and Buchanan, together with Inspector Edward F. Flanagan of the Dedham police, Custodian Apted and Superintendent Frank H. Carney of the Widener Library posed as "book buyers" before his [Williams'] three children during their long day of checking through the volumes at the Dedham home.
>
> They were volumes on all topics. There was no fiction. They ranged from weighty law tomes to biologies, books on anatomy, physiology and naval subjects.
>
> During the years that books have been mysteriously disappearing from the shelves of Widener Library, Williams has been wandering about the place, having certain privileges which were even denied to under-graduate students. He has been well known to attachés of the library.

Reporters delighted in portraying the arrest of this outwardly bookish man. The *Post* stated that when Williams "was told by police that he was to be locked up he asked if he should bring his nightshirt and asked about accommodations at the Cambridge lockup." The *Boston Traveler* further reported that Williams "appeared surprised when informed that no sheets were provided for prisoners."

Ultimately, Williams received a sentence of two years' imprisonment. His fate, in fact, was the source of Widener's infamous book plate, an example of which is pasted to the front of the clippings booklet, which reads: "This book was stolen from Harvard College Library. It was later recovered. The thief was sentenced to two years at hard labor."

But Williams's sentence did not put an end to book thievery in Widener. The *Boston Evening Transcript* reported in March 1932 that "[f]ollowing the arrest of thieves in New York who were operating on the Harvard Library and had taken rare books to the value of $40,000, Widener Library officials report that there has been a noticeable increase in the number of missing books which have been secretly returned to the library." The story concludes by describing the advent of a new feature in Widener's heretofore casual securtity system: a turnstile, "installed to prevent unauthorized taking of books has proved itself a valuable addition in spite of thc slight inconvenience it has caused students. Together with the examples made of thieves, it has been instrumental in stopping over eighty-five percent of all losses. It has stopped deliberate thefts, and prevents students from accidentally removing a volume." Though the turnstile marked a turning point in Widener's relations with the public, it would hardly stop the depredations of future biblioklepts from inside the university or from without.

IN ITS THIRD DECADE, WIDENER WAS ALREADY APPROACHING venerability; staff and administrators who had been present when it opened were fast disappearing. Eleanor Elkins Widener Rice died on 13 July 1937, ending her decades of attention to the library and her son's memorial rooms. Archibald Cary Coolidge had already retired in 1928, his place taken by Professor Robert Pierpont Blake; Alfred Claghorn Potter replaced William Coolidge Lane soon thereafter. Potter had worked in the library since 1893, specializing from the start in acquisitions. By the time of Potter's retirement, the library was acquiring thirty thousand volumes annually; the total size of the library during his career had grown from 304,000 volumes to 1,970,000. Potter retired in 1936; Blake resigned in 1937. George Parker Winship also retired as librarian of the Treasure Room in 1937–after a short and tempestuous tenure as curator of the Harry Elkins Widener collection (Eleanor had disliked his adventuresome approach to curating her son's collection) and a longer stay in the Treasure Room. He was replaced by William A. Jackson, who became Assistant Librarian for the Treasure Room and Professor of Bibliography; and Philip Hofer '21, who joined as Curator of Printing and Graphic Arts. As the Harvard College Library grew in the coming years, these two scholars would help to found the Houghton Library, which replaced the Treasure Room as Harvard's repository for rare books and manuscripts. In the absence of Potter, meanwhile, Walter Benjamin Briggs served as acting librarian (formerly he had been in charge of reference in the College Library) until the appointment of Keyes Metcalf as both Director and Librarian.

In his history of Harvard's libraries, Potter had estimated the capacity of the new library at 1,433,000 volumes; he guessed that by adding shelving in the two lower levels and tightening existing shelving, ultimate capacity could be increased to 2,200,000 books. But Widener's collections were by now well on their way to 3 million books, with no end in sight. While Widener's design was innovative in many ways, it was in practice a remarkably conservative institution. Widener, like Gore, was expected to be the chief repository of Harvard's books; like Gore, it prescribed a rather narrow set of uses for books and the other materials in its care. In this sense it was less innovative, at its opening, than the new Bryant Park home of the New York Public Library; its readers were already specialized, defined by tradition; it did not try to create new kinds of readers or fresh approaches to reading. And yet the academic approach to reading had never been a static thing, and in the middle of the twentieth century it, like so many things, was on the march. Such changes were hardly manifest in the library alone–indeed they affected every aspect of academic life. But in Widener especially, such change would exposed both

The Widener Treasure Room, which held collections that became the basis of Houghton Library. Today, this space serves as the reading room of Widener's Periodicals Department.

the resilience and the limitations of the building's design.

Into the midst of a transforming academe strode Harvard's new president, forty-year-old James Bryant Conant, as unlike A. Lawrence Lowell as Lowell had been different from Eliot. To Lowell, Harvard's modernity was bound up in the destiny of his class; while Conant's Harvard likewise pursued a destiny, it was one manifest not in the descendants of puritans and public-minded, fireside intellectuals, but in the outlines of an idealized notion of American experience. The influence of those poles that had governed life at Harvard for centuries—faith and service, honor and duty—began to recede with the rise of the can-do professionalization and practical optimism of twentieth century America.

Conant's field was chemistry, and he had distinguished himself both as an enthusiastic administrator and an inventive and indefatigable scientist. A native of Boston's Dorchester neighborhood and the son of a real estate developer, Conant was affluent but not genteel. He spent World War One in a government laboratory that produced chemical weapons, then returned to Harvard, where he had earlier distinguished himself as a student, to teach and pursue research. As department chair he set himself apart from colleagues with his zeal for administration, even as he continued to experiment and publish in his field. His ambitions, though confided only to his wife, were clear enough.

As President Lowell neared retirement, he surveyed the field of potential successors; Conant impressed him and repelled him at once. Conant differed in matters of politics; he was, in relative terms, a populist, with a view of higher education—and of Harvard's place in society—that was at once ambitious and pragmatic. Lowell by contrast was a true Brahmin, a political quietist who tolerated and furthered ethnic discrimination in housing and admissions. Typical of his class, Lowell argued confusingly that the intermingling of Jews and blacks with the dominant Anglo-Americans would lead to greater enmity and misunderstanding; concord could only be achieved if certain boundaries, discrete and durable, were maintained. Such policies and their more subtle legacies would recede under Conant, whose commitment to meritocratic standards differed fundamentally from Lowell's.

And yet Harvard after Lowell would need an energetic and innovative administrator. The university had grown dramatically: enrollment had doubled, the number of faculty had increased by an even higher percentage, the endowment had grown from $22 million to $126 million, and Widener was just one of more than sixty buildings (albeit the largest) built on Lowell's watch. Harvard had emerged from the war deeply entangled in national affairs, more engaged than ever before in research and administration in the national interest—and more dependent on government monies. A facility for bureaucracy and public relations would be required of any new president. And by 1932, with the aging Lowell openly talking retirement, the search was on.

What was more, there were similarities between Lowell and Conant. Both men were internationalists who envisioned a global role for America and for Harvard. Lowell forcefully campaigned on behalf of President Woodrow Wilson's League of Nations. Early in his adult life, Conant had dreamed of being

Secretary of State—a premonition of the role he would play in the administration of occupied Germany after World War Two. While the two men came from vastly different fields (Lowell, though he never took a Ph.D., was a leading political scientist), they shared an interest in public affairs (decades later, Lowell would give his autobiography the subtitle "Memoirs of a Social Inventor"). Conant, though not so well known as Lowell had been at the start of his presidency, was widely respected in his field and popular around Harvard as a teacher. And amidst a postwar technological boom that not even the Depression could slow, Conant's stature as a research scientist was a distinct asset.

Like his predecessors, President James Bryant Conant would take as his mandate not only the remaking of Harvard, but of higher education as well. His meritocratic university placed renewed emphasis on the practical knowledge which Thorstein Veblen had deemed the chief object of the American university in the twentieth century; Conant's university would be a place of closely coordinated functions and carefully tested methods. The librarian who administered Conant's library was prepared by upbringing and sensibility to bridge Harvard's new synthesis of tradition and innovation. Keyes Dewitt Metcalf was the first professionally trained librarian to head the University Library, as well as the first both to lead the University Library as Director and manage Widener as Librarian of Harvard College.

By Keyes Metcalf's arrival in 1937, the mongrel nature of the university library was becoming apparent. Widener's mandate was essentially the same as that of Gore Hall, but the university had changed dramatically. The suite of functions planned for Widener—research library, teaching collection, study space, rare books repository, university archives—was growing in number and in its demands on space. Under Metcalf, these functions would peel off into new libraries, even as Widener's remaining functions were increasingly specialized, sequestered, and compartmentalized. This was Conant's university, meritocratic and professionalized; it was a vision Metcalf was uniquely well-suited to implement.

Widener in 1937 had presented the incoming Metcalf with a host of challenges. Chief among these was lack of space; College Library collections had grown from six hundred thousand to some two million bound volumes by this time, and the shelves were full. And yet Widener's sheer size, the enormity of its gift, and its identification with a single donor made replacing it politically, financially, and symbolically impossible. And in any case, Harvard's library needs had become greater than any one library could fulfill. The importance of club libraries and the student-managed library in the Harvard Union had decreased with the centralization of library work under Arhibald Cary Coolidge; now, the whole of the university depended on Widener, and the library was cracking under the pressure to acquire exponentially increasing stocks of books. Metcalf estimated that Widener's replacement would need to contain five million square feet of space—dwarfing Widener, already Harvard's largest building at 320,000 square feet. The cost, not to mention the impact of such a building on the Yard, would be staggering.

Widener in the thirties, its ivy-covered walls concealing overcrowded stacks and overburdened reading rooms.

What he termed the conservative choice—building a new library—was thus effectively closed to Metcalf. And so over the course of his long tenure, he would adopt the far more innovative approach of building a host of specialized new libraries to relieve the pressure Widener was under. Widener, for its part, would become radically specialized; first, as the home of research collections in the humanities and social sciences; second, as the administrative hub of an increasingly decentralized college library system, which included libraries like Lamont and Houghton. More space in Widener would be devoted to the needs of an ever-growing staff. Over the next few decades, reading rooms would be cubicled and cordoned off; whole zones of the library would disappear behind closed doors, becoming ever more mysterious even to Widener habitués among the faculty and the student body. In the reading rooms, Metcalf would strive to make Widener into a modern "research center" by concentrating reading light: painting nearly every surface white; adding reflective dropped ceilings; and filling work spaces and reading rooms with the harsh, oscillatory glow of fluorescent light.

In the long run, Metcalf's struggle with the building preserved Widener; without his reforms, the library would undoubtedly have come down sooner or later. And yet his changes also fought the building's original charms: its rococo interior, its internal unity, and especially its character as a great public space and nerve center for the university. These changes proceeded apace with the transformation of Harvard as a whole in the forties and fifties into a more meritocratic and professionalized place. They also set the stage for the shattering clash of cultures that took place in the sixties, the shocks of which would be felt in and around Widener for decades afterward.

Born on April 13, 1889, Keyes Metcalf was the second-youngest of eighteen children. Although his parents were devoted to their children—his father had retired early from his railroad career to spend more time with his family—they had a lot on their hands. Keyes would have enjoyed little time with them before their deaths, which occurred early in his childhood: his mother in his seventh year, his father in his tenth. Among the half-siblings and other relatives who cared for young Keyes after his parents' deaths was Anna Metcalf Root, an older half-sister whose husband, Azariah Smith Root, was Oberlin College Librarian. The Metcalfs' tie to Oberlin was close—all but one of Keyes's brothers attended (his sisters, all of whom also attended college, went East for their education). Metcalf spent the rest of his childhood on the Oberlin campus, eventually graduating from the college in 1911. His library career had begun somewhat earlier; from the age of thirteen, his uncle employed him as a page at a starting wage of five cents an hour. Although active as a student and an athlete at Oberlin, Metcalf spent a great deal of time in the stack. After graduation he went to New York, where he entered the library school at New York Public and rose to Chief of Stacks in the library. His prescient thesis topic, "Administration of a Large Library Stack," prefigured the concerns of his later career at Harvard.

Metcalf's appointment itself marked a watershed moment in Harvard's library history. Metcalf was the first Harvard librarian to have received professional training, and one of the few to have been appointed from outside of Harvard. In giving the choice their imprimatur, Conant and the Corporation indicated a desire for Harvard's libraries to join the wider world of librarianship—just as Harvard as a whole was increasingly professionalized and open to the wide world.

Over nearly two decades, Metcalf's sweeping changes would alter the course of the Harvard College Library as much as the building of Widener itself had done. Like Conant with the university as a whole, Metcalf's first challenge was to bring a rampant system to administrative heel. And yet he hardly checked the library's riotous growth; instead, he husbanded it to greater feats of expansion. Williams points out that "[d]uring the eighteen Metcalf years the University Library increased by more than 2,000,000 volumes and pamphlets.... it is interesting to observe that this is twice as many as were added during the eighteen years of Archibald Cary Coolidge's directorship, which is remembered as the golden age of collecting." As Williams admits, the comparison is not entirely fair: Coolidge's collecting strategies, which

Keyes Dewitt Metcalf

were as innovative as they were massively acquisitive, pointed the way for collection-building in the years to come. But then, Metcalf's additions and innovations were hardly restricted to collections. He altered every aspect of life in the library.

In a previous generation, Coolidge had set the library on a new path, away from the library as a kind of intellectual general store and toward the research collection, at once broad in scope and deep in comprehensiveness, that would serve Harvard's shift toward professionalism. Subsequent administrators carried on in the Coolidge vein, building increasingly powerful and dynamic research collections. But Widener had been built to the a la carte specifications of Gore Hall, intended to provide "one-stop shopping" for the bibliographical needs of student and faculty alike. Practically speaking, the majority of its public space was taken up with service to undergraduates, especially the administration of complex systems of books reserved for courses. And yet these same systems, rather than promoting the students' use of books, actively discouraged it instead. Between subtle and ramified collections and a student body possessing increasing intellectual sophistication stood a bureaucracy of tables, chairs, delivery desks, and loan limits, punctuated by the locked doors of a closed stack.

By the time Metcalf arrived in Widener, its collections had tripled from the 600,000 volumes it contained in 1915 to more than 1,800,000 books. The strain of growth affected faculty, staff, and students, whose complaints about the library had reached a fever pitch. In October 1937, the *Crimson* called the library "an uncongenial colossus devoid of all human warmth." Elsewhere, the *Crimson* noted that most undergraduates didn't study in Widener unless they had to, citing long lines, indifferent access, and poor treatment. The lighting was also bad: Trumbauer's placement of the reading room on the north side of the building, while it served his design for the Memorial Rooms and the grand entrance on the Yard, deprived readers of afternoon light, and *Crimson* editorial writers bemoaned the inadequate, flickering lamps. More troubling was the feeling that undergraduates took third place in priority behind faculty and graduate students. Even students writing honors theses typically were restricted to ten trips into the stack per year, despite the fact that "if allowed to work without obstruction they might make worthwhile contributions to their fields." The article joined the ranks of library critics since time immemorial when it railed at the "implicit" and "official argument . . . that when the public handles the books they are mislaid and inefficiency results." In an editorial letter, a *Crimson* reader described the situation met by his tutor when he tried to find books in Widener:

> Three years ago [he] guilelessly slipped three cards into the hands of the attendant. Three books he wanted. In time, which we hesitate to define in its Widenerian concept, he was informed that there was no report of them. Then the Widener Beast sat up on its hind legs, smoothed its scales, and smilingly queried, "May we trace the books and send you a card?" The spider could no better entice the fly. "Please,"

our tutor answered. Every month now he returns to the lair with the same three cards and receives the same benign reply. But the Beast has never sent him a card. Some thirty times our tutor has baited it, but the prey eludes the trap. Mournfully we suspect that somewhere in Widener even now there is a modified Jonah who has been prowling around the bowels of the Beast for three years, encouraged at the beginning of every month by only three cards, like those he got the month before. It is a sad tale, but our tutor tells it with a smile.

Students were fed up with Widener—fed up with its inability to put needed books in their hands; fed up with the forms and cards and the lectures and all the *in loco parentis* business of rules and regulations which, in the words of another *Crimson* article, make the student feel as if "by his negligence he has jeopardized the future of Harvard College." Some noticed that Widener's innumerable special libraries, far from providing convenient access to collections in special subjects, actually frustrated the student pur-

A crowd of students faces the Delivery Desk crush.

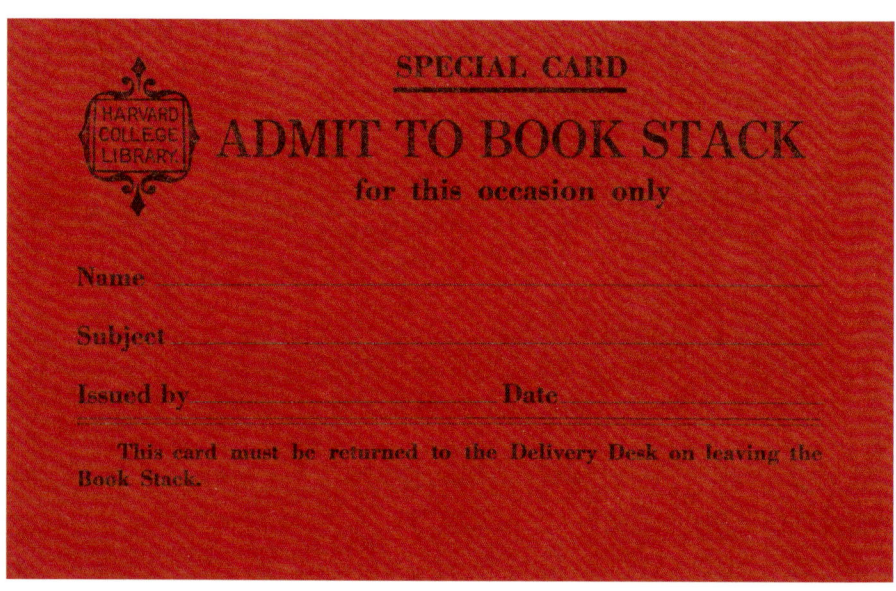

One of several kinds of cards issued to allow special—and limited—access to the stacks.

suing advanced coursework. "[T]he whole study of music is checked by an inaccessible library hidden in one of the basements of Widener," the *Crimson* complained, while in the field of education it found that "this [department's] library, considered one of the best of its kind, must remain in the depths of Widener, suffering from disuse, deserving separate housing." Meanwhile the progressive *Harvard Monthly*, looking into labor conditions in the library, complained that while Depression-era Harvard could find fifty thousand dollars to place two bronze rhinoceroses in front of the biological laboratories, it could afford to pay Widener stack pages little more than forty dollars a month—an amount which, though in line with wages elsewhere, the *Monthly* considered less than a living wage. And even at this low wage, the *Monthly* argued, Widener only retained three full-time pages— hardly a large enough staff to meet the students' crushing appetite for books. Collegians were frustrated by and all but excluded from a place that claimed the mantle of "finest college library in the world."

In the midst of empowering changes throughout the university, and almost without anyone noticing, Widener had become imperiled. A mere two decades after it opened, changes in its uses, in the complexion of its staff and patrons, and in the growth of its collection, threatened it with sudden obsolescence. Students especially were turning away in droves—and increasingly, with the library in the Student Union and the house libraries (supplied by Widener purchases) to rely on, were finding that they could all but do without the "uncongenial colossus."

So Metcalf would have to manage Widener in a way that would not merely sustain it, but transform it. Under Metcalf, Widener would grow into a specialized research library while maintaining its place as the practical and one might almost say the spiritual core of Harvard's growing library system. Metcalf strove both to foster change, and to constrain it, to build the library into a complex and efficient machine that would ferry ever more books into the hands of ever more readers while at the same time dampening and containing the shocks of social changes—changes in the complexion of the university community. And so even where Metcalf resisted change, he would lay the groundwork for it.

Those who followed Metcalf's tenure in Widener would find themselves armed with tools they needed to throw the library doors—and the stacks—open to more readers than ever before. And those readers, meanwhile, with needs either too specialized or too diffuse for Widener's massive collections, found new libraries built for them close by. Once both the symbolic and the practical center of the reading experience at Harvard, Widener had been left a shell of its former self—lit by fluorescent tubes, its once-grand spaces carved into warrens of cubicles, its patrons increasingly deprived of the often confusing, occasionally serendipitous riot of associations it had promoted. Widener, for all its improvements, became unmoored.

Metcalf jumped straightaway into a comprehensive program of reform. Everything needed fixing: in Metcalf's first contribution to Harvard's *Annual Report*, he mentions that he finds fault even in the methods used for counting the books. Yet this is merely symptomatic of wider troubles. "The Widener building has now been in use for twenty-three years," he writes. "While it is customary to say in moving into a new building that it will provide for one hundred years' growth, it is unusual for a library not to be outgrown in twenty or twenty-five years; and it is not surprising that the space situation in Widener is becoming critical." Metcalf notes that the "Union Catalogue has overflowed into the corridor on the main floor, and will naturally, as time goes on, require more room." In his first year's report Metcalf concludes on a demure note, stating that "The Director will be glad to receive suggestions from those interested" in helping to determine "the future program of the Library." And yet amid his careful statistics, there could be no mistaking the scope of the problem. With the addition of 35,000 volumes and pamphlets, the main collection of the Harvard College Library in that year (1937-8) grew to 1,816,700. In its first twenty-three years, Widener had reached its capacity, with no end of growth in sight.

Metcalf's prosaic, pragmatic description of Widener's troubles in the *Annual Report* differed starkly from the tone the President took. In his introduction, Conant adopted a ruminative, "aims of education" approach, indicating that his concern lay not with Harvard, but with the growing nation that supplied its students. He noted "profound changes" which had taken place in the meaning and complexion of American education over the previous four decades. "Today we all realize that democracy is not a self-perpetuating virus adapted to any body politic," he writes, but a "special type of organism requiring specific nutrient materials." In 1898, Conant reports, barely ten percent of American youth attended secondary school; by 1936, that percentage had increased to sixty-five—and that in a nation in which the total number of youth, according to Conant, had increased dramatically, from about six hudred thousand to over six million. For Harvard, Conant argued that such changes necessitated a rethinking of the aims and means of its curriculum, to make it responsive to the "varied vocational channels through which . . . graduates will ultimately contribute to the national welfare" while maintaining the capacity to produce men and women "who shall be truly learned in the great heritage of our civilization."

Conant's administration was characterized by such cogitation, and in Keyes Metcalf he found a librarian who could combine narrowly focused administration with wide-ranging, creative philosophizing. Beneath their bland practicality, Metcalf's early pronouncements on the state of the library gave but subtle clues to the rethinking and transformation he would undertake in the decades to come. But immediately, two chief problems were apparent: Widener's mongrel nature, and its critical lack of space. He realized that both represented new challenges for Harvard as well as for the library community at large.

Metcalf's vision was austere, but it was also ambitious and comprehensive; it promised sweeping changes for the Harvard College Library—the building of new libraries for rare books and undergraduate work and a storage site for Harvard's rapidly growing collection—changes that would determine the character of Widener for the rest of the century. At the root of these changes was Metcalf's insight that Widener was insupportably diverse in design and mission. In building a library that would serve as teaching collection, research library, rare books repository, workplace and study space, Coolidge, Trumbauer, and the Elkins-Wideners had indisputably created a great library—indeed, perhaps *too* great a library.

Beyond expansive plans for new buildings, Metcalf pursued small-scale changes in staffing and service that together gave Harvard's libraries a new lease on life. The reference service, for instance, was understaffed, underutilized, and not well tuned to the needs of students. In his memoir, Metcalf would later recollect the effect of such conditions on student use of Widener:

> The following incident may suggest the sort of thing that happened far too often. A student checked the catalog; after long effort, because there were thousands of cards under Shakespeare, he found a card for *Hamlet*, which he wanted, and turned in a call-slip for it. He had naturally selected the first copy of *Hamlet* listed; since all the cards were arranged by date of publication, the copy he requested was so valuable that it was kept in the rare-book collection and not ordinarily made available to undergraduates. He was told that the library had other copies, and that he should look it up again and turn in another call-slip. This time he made his way to the last of cards for *Hamlet* and requested the most recent edition; this, of course, turned out to be in use by another student. It was then suggested that he go to the stack himself,

and he was directed to the area devoted to Shakespeare. Instead of the catalog's thousands of cards for Shakespeare, he found scores of shelves of books, and decided that it would not be worthwhile to search through them to find what he wanted. He left the building without being told that, if he had simply asked for a copy of *Hamlet*, one would undoubtedly have been made available.

Spurred by such conundrums, Metcalf moved swiftly, changing what he could by fiat while laying the groundwork for larger alterations by publishing, planning, and cementing his ties with President Conant. Students quickly noticed changes. On 4 November 1937, the *Crimson* observed that "While the general student body might not be alert enough to realize it, Widener Library has been making steps forward in the last few weeks toward the eventual goal of providing genuinely adequate service to the undergraduates. Not least of the factors making for improvement has been the realization on the part of those who are responsible for Widener's destiny that the students are vitally interested in their collection of books...." The article went on to point out two particular student resentments in need of redress: the month-long loan periods for books leading to delays in access to especially high-demand titles and the flagrant difference in policy toward overdue books for students versus faculty. In relatively short order, Metcalf would move to change these policies and a host of others touching every aspect of life in the library. By 1939, Metcalf announced that "[t]he borrowing period for students in the College Library has been reduced from a month to two weeks, and in cases of books in demand to one week. This change has naturally resulted in a more rapid turnover of books, and in my opinion and that of Mr. Mahady, Superintendent of the Reading Room, should make it possible, and in many cases desirable, to leave in the stack room, subject to the regular borrowing rules, books that have in the past been reserved in the Reading Room for use within the building, or for overnight use only."

Meanwhile, Metcalf sought reductions in dependence on reserve books, both to cut down on staff time spent in their administration and to free up more books for lending. He wrote a letter to faculty asking them to scrutinize reserve lists and return to the stacks books no longer needed for coursework. The *Crimson* had hailed Metcalf's reforms; faculty were less enthusiastic. D. W. Prall of Leverett House replied to Metcalf's survey by noting that while he thought the shorter loan period "is a very good idea; and although I wish you would apply it to faculty, who are the great offenders in my experience," he doubted he could modify his reserve list, which includes "only the more complete forms of the writings that I require students to read." Douglas Bush wrote that "the genus student remains much the same, and two out of three are likely to postpone most of their collateral reading to the last few weeks or even a shorter time . . . . [and] the borrowing of a book for two weeks or even one will not help when one or two students want the same books within the same week." Kenneth B. Murdock, meanwhile, noted that the reserve shelves permit browsing, which is unavailable due to closed stacks (a point he does not make, but was nonetheless the case). "Often," he pointed out, "a man can learn a good deal in fifteen minutes or half an hour spent just looking through the books on the reserved shelf, and I think this opportunity is a valuable part of the arrangements for any course." Not everyone objected. Some, recognizing the problematic nature of reserves, preferred to arrange for students to acquire the books they needed. French professor André Morize, for instance, reported that he had "piled up in the past few years, a fairly large collection of French texts in very inexpensive editions, offering the students for works they have to read, a number of copies that varies from ten to fifty or more." Others, however, were neither so sanguine nor so generous. Prof. Derwent Whittlesley of Geology and Geography: "It has been my experience that the only way to get undergraduates to read books is to put them where they will fall over them." And increasing pressure on library staff by increasing the frequency with which books were charged out could result in disaster. "For libraries," he wrote, "apparently are compelled by tradition to have such cheap help that there is inevitable inefficiency."

Metcalf soldiered on. He argued that the closed reserve system "demands a much greater seating capacity with the attendant heavy overhead expenses. The open reserve system is appreciated by the students because it allows a much freer use of the books. By eliminating the bargain basement aspect of the loan desk for reserves the tone of the library is improved." Ultimately, however, faculty clamor over Metcalf's intitiative rose until, according to a letter written to Prof. Theodore Morrison, he decided that he did not "wish to press the matter" any further. This would not be the last time Metcalf clashed with faculty.

In any case, Metcalf knew that Widener's troubles were bigger than the system of reserve books. His overriding concern was the bane of all libraries: lack of space. As early as April 1939, Metcalf was restlessly coaxing proposals for vast additions out of colleagues and architects. A memo in Metcalf's papers outlines one such plan:

> After discussing various proposals for enlarging the Library in the Yard by underground connections with Widener and the building of additional buildings connected with bridges, the following plan seemed best.
>
> It was proposed to build an underground library of some 200,000 cubic feet running in the general direction of the President's House from the Widener Library and connecting with the basement of a new library building to be built on the site of the Gummere house. This building would be of considerable height and approximately tower shaped with a maximum total cubic feet of 5,000. . . . The cost would be estimated at $5,000,000 with an additional million dollars as endowment for physical maintenance. If it were possible to build such a building with the connection just mentioned, it is estimated that the expansion of the library could be handled until 1969.

The numbers proposed here are astonishing. Widener in its vastness contained less than 320,000 square feet of usable space; the library Metcalf envisioned to meet Harvard's needs would equal fifteen Wideners. It would mean building a skyscraper in the Yard. Metcalf realized the impracticality of such a scheme—and as he did, the monumental challenge he faced became clear.

Metcalf soon began to define the problem in terms that would shape the course of growth in the Harvard College Library for the next fifty years. If he couldn't practically build up, forging a massive library tower in one stroke, then he would have to grow the library outward and downward in phases. The work would begin with a series of shifts in the collections which, while modest in themselves, would chart a new, decentralized course. Options included the movement of books in government, economics, and public documents to Littauer and elsewhere; newspapers, comic books, and education collections also could be moved from Widener, whose resulting collections would focus more closely on the humanities and social sciences.

But movement of books was only half the problem: challenges remained in access to books as well as space for readers and staff. "It should be added," Metcalf wrote, "that by [shifting collections] the present unsatisfactory situation in the Widener building would be continued."

> The center of the work in Widener is on the second floor, fully thirty feet above street level; the charging desk is at one end of what might be called a ribbon of books, . . . and it has a connection, not with the center of the stack, but with the eighth of ten levels; the stack is without modern machinery for book handling; the toilet facilities are hopelessly inadequate and poorly located; the congested workrooms cost the University considerable sums annually; and the facilities for students and faculty are not up to standard . . . .
>
> The Widener building is today congested and inadequate, but by the use of various expedients, . . . it will be possible, although unsatisfactory, to continue in the present building as headquarters of the College Library for from eight to ten years.

Metcalf considered his options. He could assign more of the existing space in Widener to books, crowding out staff and readers; alternatively, he could try adding on to Widener, building annexes connected by bridges or underground tunnels. Such annexes could be constructed in phases, as the need—and the funds—emerged over time. The increased space for books and readers on campus could be complemented with a remote warehouse where little-used volumes could be stored—hearkening back to President Eliot's notions about "dead books." Of course, such measures would stir controversy. The terms of the Widener gift made the construction of additions to the building all but impossible, and the idea of storing large numbers of books off-site would be loathed by faculty. In fact, Metcalf would make his move in amazingly short time: within three years he would have a specialized center for rare books scholarship in Houghton Library, a warehouse for off-site storage of collections in the New England Depository, and the beginnings of a plan for a first-of-its-kind undergraduate library, Lamont. But from the vantage point of 1939 the challenges were huge, even for the quietly formidable Metcalf.

KEYES DEWITT METCALF, HOWEVER, WAS NOT THE ONLY formidable presence in Widener during the 1930s and '40s. At the time of his arrival, the cataloging department was headed by T. Frank Currier, a proud and diligent scholar and an administrator as restlessly domineering as he was appreciative of his staff's hard work. As Widener's collections had grown, so had its staff of cataloguers, by and large women, who quietly, under Currier's constant encouragement, transformed their duties from clerical routine into the exacting, specialized, para-academic profession that cataloguing has become.

In memoranda to the newly-arrived Metcalf, Currier comes across as punctilious and proud, but also protective of his staff and their rights and eager to promote their opportunities. When he writes Metcalf on behalf of a long-time member of his staff, he argues that she should be given special consideration and awarded a retirement package equal to half her pay—this at a time when retirement for wage-earning staff, and especially for women, was a precarious enterprise.

Currier appreciates the linguistic exertions of his staff, many of whom become adept at foreign languages and orthographies in the course of their work. He lobbies for giving staff members time and, if possible, financial support to pursue graduate work of potential benefit to their work in the library, noting that several of these women have made themselves into able linguists whom he relies on to pursue subtle cataloging problems throughout Widener's far-ranging collections. He distinguishes such staff members, most of whom worked many years in Widener, from the less-trained clerical workers in his department—a distinction that Harvard was hard pressed to make among the many women in university employment. But even for those women doing relatively less skilled labor Currier favored liberal and flexible policies that emphasized their dignity as working persons. In 1938, Currier tells Metcalf

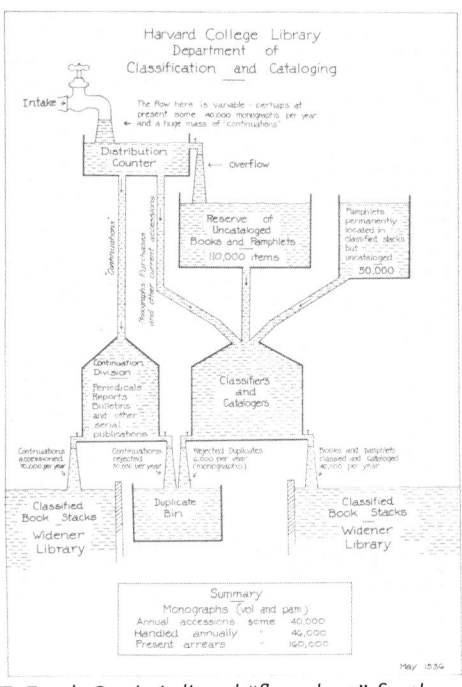

T. Frank Currier's literal "flow chart" for the Department of Classification and Cataloging.

> that (while) there is no necessity of giving to all our clerical workers the full four weeks vacation which is desirable for the workers of a so-called professional grade . . . it seems to me desirable to make exception for certain workers of long standing and excellent record who are in the semi-professional grade and receiving good pay. . . . [I]t is, however, highly desirable, and it would seem to us wholly practicable, to make an arrangement whereby clerical workers add one hour a week to their services during the winter and take the four weeks vacation. The plan . . . was successful. . . . [But it] was discontinued automatically when a change was made in the number of hours service for the whole staff, this change being made suddenly without discussion so far as I know.

Currier contrasts the salaries of highly trained women on his staff to workers with comparable experience; he quotes the prices of annuities the library could purchase to augment meagre university retirement payments; he argues for longer and more flexible vacations. And he showed concern not only for the status of his staff, but for their working conditions as well. In an 11 April

1938 report, Currier called for sweeping reorganization of staff space for cataloguing and allied work, recommending that staff for "ordering, classification, cataloging, and the like be removed to the upper floor with the Union Catalog in the corridor, where could be found room also for numerous desks," that the former librarians' office be repurposed for serials or for cataloging, noting that the current arrangement "sadly decentralizes staff and causes time to be lost traveling in the elevator or waiting while others travel therein."

But in all things Currier could be prickly, especially over questions of cataloguing practice or what he saw as his own professional prerogatives. In a letter to to a member of the American Library Association's Catalogue Code Committee, Currier gives vent to his frustration with changes in cataloging standards:

> Here is a belated, but not too late, afterthought. How many librarians really approve the tendency still evident among catalogers of over-decapitalization? Is it not an appropriate time to call a halt? Of course it will be said that we cannot change a long established custom like this and someone will point to the millions of cards that have been printed under the old rules. It seems to me high time that we stop writing names of organized bodies thus: "Iowa hornets' nest brigade association." It ought to be 'Iowa Hornets' Nest Brigade Association," wherever used, whether in title or heading.
>
> Secondly, how many librarians would prefer to capitalize German nouns?

But Currier was by no means mired in the minutiae of his craft; as a supervisor, he was as engaged and supportive as he could be demanding. Currier's attitude toward women was unusual at Harvard–particularly in Widener, which was an especially unwelcoming a place for women, be they staff, student, or scholar. Women had faced problems in the building almost from the day it opened. As a letter dated 18 August 1915 shows, they sometimes petitioned Mrs. Widener herself for attention:

> I hope very greatly that these words will come to your personal attention, for I write of a matter which concerns the dignity and convenience of every woman scholar who will in the

coming years make use of the Widener Memorial Library.

May I tell you since it is much more than an individual thing, of the feeling of reverence, of serious joy and pride, with which I went there a few days ago? I have worked in many of the great libraries abroad, but the knowledge of them served only to quicken the feeling with which, as an American, I looked on this new great house of scholarship.

You will understand from this something of the reversal of feeling that followed when I was informed later, first by two young women assistants in the Catalogue Room and finally by the person in charge of that room which seems, as it were, the shrine of the whole building, that in all the immense place there was no Womens Room—only that for the staff which they said was not "open to the public." This last person added the ineffably stupid comment, "You know this is a college boys' library."

It is not simply a plea for a convenience which is a matter of course in any large institutional building which I send you. It is a plea that through the Harvard University officials who will harken to you if to anyone in this matter, some insistent command should be set before its subordinates to the effect that the women scholars who come to the Widener Library should not be made to feel as interlopers in a "boys' school." Whatever be the problems of undergraduate co-education, surely it is an insult to a great sanctuary of knowledge that any sex distinctions should be made among mature and independent investigators. Personally I acknowledge the courtesy in the past of the higher officials of the University Library, but in the new building they seem to be less accessible than in the old. It is of persons in the places of apparent authority, as, for instance, the person in charge of the Widener room, that I speak. [signed] Laura A. Hibbard

But despite such pleas, the concerns of women in Widener were routinely dismissed, as this 1941 letter to Metcalf from Stanley Salmen of the Harvard Summer School demonstrates:

Enclosed are some comments from an obviously sensitive woman member of the Summer School of last year. Nevertheless, her remark about tables in Widener soiling dress fronts may have some merit that should be considered

A flag used to segregate books for women readers in Widener's Radcliffe study.

by the cleaning people in Widener. It is probably a consideration that has not occurred to them, inasmuch as Harvard students would not be similarly bothered.

If you think it wise, you may like to call to your staff's attention the statement made on the back of the sheet. The general tone of the lady's remarks, however, probably indicate[d] that she has exaggerated whatever she may have chanced to have overheard. It is such little things, though, that may influence a student to go to some other Summer School rather than Harvard, inasmuch as many students have little basis on which to choose a Summer School and are guided sometimes by trivial remarks of their friends.

While Metcalf and his male colleagues adopted dismissive tones in their consideration of such complaints, women of all ranks were forced to petition Metcalf for reasonable access to the library, as shown by this letter received by Metcalf's office in December 1940:

I have just heard that women may receive from you permission to work in Widener evenings. This is very encouraging, for I have often wanted to do work in Widener after six o'clock but have, as a mat-

Two women process recently received journals in Widener's order department ca. 1950.

> ter of course, given up the thought of doing so. Now that the rule has changed, I should like very much to have your permission to use Widener evenings.
>
> I have a Corporation appointment as Assistant Professor at the Business School. My work is in Business History in the department headed by Professor Gras. [signed] Henrietta M. Larson

Metcalf granted Professor Larson evening access. It is astonishing, however, that someone with faculty rank would even have had to petition for an accommodation so basic to scholarly life. Of course, before the change in policy to which Larson refers, she would not have been allowed in Widener after hours at all. And despite this relative easing of access, other women with legitimate interest in using Widener were not so lucky as Larson. Metcalf routinely turned away Radcliffe students and outside researchers; only the comparatively senior appointment of Ms. Larson stood her in good stead. A professor wrote Metcalf on 12

Colossus 113

February 1941 to request access for a Radclifffe student enrolled in his seminar. "Since she has afternoon classes almost every day of the week," Leopold writes, "I feel that she would be placed under a serious handicap, in relation to the other members of the seminar, if she did not have access to Widener for long hours of uninterrupted research in the evenings. . . . This case is a forerunner, I would guess, of the many applications you will receive next year when all course Primarily for Graduate Students will be opened to Radcliffe students." Metcalf refused the request, though he acknowledged that Leopold is likely right in forecasting many more such requests, and that the library may well be forced to liberalize access in the future.

Women faced uphill climbs in every aspect of life in the library. Whether patrons or staff, women had to leave the building by six o'clock in the evening, and Radcliffe students were long restricted to their tiny chamber, separated from the main reading room with its extensive reference books and services. Even the ever-present problem of inadequate lavatories worked to deny functional access to women—patrons requesting directions to a women's restroom were routinely misled, denied access, or simply told that such things do not exist at a college for men such as Harvard. Aside from the occasional student or scholar, Widener remained hostile to women—especially, perhaps, to those on its staff, who had grown accustomed to patronizing official admonitions as this one, in a 1948 memorandum from Metcalf's office:

> Please remind all women on your staff that they are expected to leave the building after working hours. An exception to this rule is permitted when evening meetings make a suitable waiting room desirable. In these cases the Staff Lunch Room is available until 7 P.M.
>
> As the Library is not open to women readers after 6 P.M. without special permission, it is in the interests of good management that members of the staff follow suit.

Of course, gender discrimination was not due to Metcalf's predilections alone. Harvard was slow to change. Reflecting on the Harvard College Library's treatment of women staff, Paul H.

Buck later noted that, the work of T. Frank Currier notwithstanding, Harvard took its time recognizing the contribution of women to the library world:

> [W]omen were to form a large proportion of all professional librarians, and it was inevitable that they should eventually do much of the professional work in the Harvard University Library. But . . . recognition of their professional status was slow to come. Lillian A. Hall, Custodian of the Theatre Collection from 1925 to 1940, was the first woman librarian to have an appointment as an officer of the University, and no woman in the Library had such an appointment for a year following her retirement. Then, in 1941, the Librarian of the Fogg Art Museum received one. There were three by the end of 1955, and three were added in 1957; and a total of eight women were officers of the Library during the first half of 1958 on.

Inevitably, women in the library were called upon to play roles other than those they carved out as catalogers, curators, and able linguists. On social occasions, they were expected to act as hostesses. In the early nineteen-forties, staff at Widener banded together to organize a series of staff teas. "A charge of 25 cents a month will be made," the announcement read. "For the present we shall have to ask each person to provide his own tea-cup, which may be kept in the lunchroom."

While both men and women staff members participated, contributing funds to purchase cups and saucers, tea, pastries, and precious sugar (which wartime rationing made scarce), women were expected to organize these affairs. Eventually, however, the "Tea committee"—made up by Milda E. Conlan, Margaret Currier, and Catherine C. Rinker—recorded in their notes that "[w]e have not started our usual afternoon tea sessions this year because of the increasing unwillingness of some members of the staff to serve as hostess." Ultimately, they decided to hire a Radcliffe student to act as hostess, although this raised the price of participating in the tea for men and women alike.

While Metcalf strove to maintain Widener as a bastion of separation of the sexes, the changing world continued to intrude on the ordered life of the library. In the late thirties,

European intellectuals were seeking refuge from the rise of fascism; Harvard, like many American universities, was wary of political entanglement, and administrators strove to rein in departments that reached out to refugees. Metcalf was open to the hiring of foreign scholars as librarians and curators, but worried that the university would look unfavorably on such hires. On 21 December 1938, Metcalf received a letter from Conant regarding the employment of "refugee" professors: none are to be employed until a formal policy is formulated. Metcalf pressed forward, however, writing Conant on 2 February 1939:

> We had correspondence with you last month about Dr. Arnold Weinberger, a German refugee who is now in Italy. Dr. Weinberger has had some experience as a librarian and more as a bookseller with rare book concerns in Germany, Austria, and Italy. We need a man of his scholarship and ability in connection with our Treasure Room cataloguing. Mr Hofer [Philip Hofer, the Widener Treasure Room's Curator of Printing and Graphic Arts] is prepared to pay him a salary of $100 a month for the nine months from October 1, 1939 to the end of the fiscal year, June 30, 1940. It should be added that if Dr. Weinberger is able to come into the country, neither the Library nor Mr Hofer will be under any special obligation in connection with him because a Dr Levy of New York has already signed an affidavit that he will be responsible for Dr. Weinberger's not becoming a public charge during the next three years....

In this case, finally, Conant gave Metcalf permission to hire Weinberger.

In time, the war effected Widener as profoundly as it impacted every aspect of American life. In April of 1941–eight months before the attack on Pearl Harbor–Conant, worried about the security of Widener's collections, directed Metcalf to make plans to move precious library and archive materials to safer premises in case of national emergency. Metcalf suggested the basement of the new Museum building at the Harvard Forest in rural Petersham, Massachusetts, adding that supplies should be stockpiled and shelving built at the site.

In a memo to staff dated 22 October 1942, Metcalf mentions that in part due to the war, help has been reduced in the stacks, and that as a result "the books in many sections of the stack have become badly mixed up . . . . It has been suggested that large numbers of the regular library staff might be willing to volunteer to stay an extra hour one or more nights a week for a limited period in an attempt to improve conditions."

But staff who went to war were not forgotten. Metcalf himself kept up a lively correspondence with a number of men, many of whom served the library in quite junior positions, who had been drafted into or volunteered for service in World War Two. Notes in Metcalf's papers list as many as twenty-nine "Widener Men in the Armed Forces"—as well as one woman, who joined the Naval Auxillary, and with whom Metcalf also strove to stay in contact. For the most part, though, his correspondents were college-age men with an interest in library work. Most of these Widener staff were given clerical work in the armed forces; others, however, saw combat in Italy, the Pacific, and elsewhere. Whether they arrive typed on green paper, handwritten on Christmas cards, or in the cramped photostats of the Government-sponsored "V-Mail," they all sought plaintively for news from home.

Sgt. Roland Moody had helped John Shea run the Widener stack. He wrote Metcalf from Camp Hale in Colorado, telling him that another librarian had joined his unit and relating details of camp life—skiing through the middle of the night, early rising, etc. Metcalf replied: "I am very glad that you wrote on March 4th. I was beginning to wonder what had happened to you. I am glad that you can be in interesting country since you have had to stay in the same place for so long, and it is fine that you have a fellow librarian near at hand at present." He goes on to update him about library staff and changes.

Others, meanwhile, wrote from the war's more exotic locales. Francis Keough, who had been an assistant in the Archives, himself a Corporal doing library work or record management—a pedestrian enough assignment, until he was sent to North Africa to do it. He wrote to tell Metcalf on 24 March 1944 about the countryside, about rural mosques and foreign legion garrisons.

> Never have I seen such wide open spaces. Pastoral, I guess, is the word for it. Along the route, we had to stop frequently to let flocks of sheep and goats pass . . . . Here and there up the sides

of hills and mountains are olive groves . . . . About every half hour we passed through small Arab settlements or French towns. These are all very dirty little places . . . . Most of the inhabitants seem rather sleepy and detached from the war-conscious world.

On April 3, Metcalf wrote, "Your fine long letter of March 20th arrived on the first of April. Just twelve days coming. I was very much interested in it."

Robert L. Work, meanwhile, who was serving as a Pharmacist's Mate aboard the U.S.S. *Canberra*, dispatched a note to Metcalf from the Pacific. "[T]he climate here," he writes, "is very enervating . . . I'd be glad for a change of temperature." He notes that news from his Widener coworkers is, "as you must know, most welcome to me." Metcalf answers with news of the New England Depository: "Things are certainly booming over there. . . . Harvard's second floor is practically full, and . . . . The Boston Public Library has finally begun to pour its books into the basement, and the time is not very far distant when we shall be pressed for space."

Cpl. Elmer Grieder wrote on 1 June 1944 that his "work is very important and interesting, tho it will take me to a theater of operations for which I have no fancy." Metcalf replied on 5 June—unbeknownst to him, of course, the eve of D-Day—telling Grieder that his "letter of June 1st has just arrived. In the same mail came a note from the Dean saying that you had been appointed by the Corporation for another three-year term as Assistant Librarian in the Graduate School of Public Administration, and that your leave of absence has been extended for the duration of your appointment if that is necessary. So at least that is one thing you needn't worry about." Grieder next writes in August, from Australia: "I'm overseas now . . . one of the quickest trips on record. It was a pleasant one, which isn't usual for Army excursions. My work is extremely interesting . . . . One officer here had a Littauer fellowship, but was drafted before he could take it." On 29 August, Metcalf replied with a rare intimate detail: "My son Gerry was in Australia for nearly a year before he went north . . . the latest word from him came from Dutch New

Guinea"—which is where Grieder himself would soon be headed.

Occasionally, news was grim. On 8 December 1944, an unnamed assistant wrote Metcalf about the location and fate of another Widener staffer in the service:

> Lt. John Gleason's address is:
> Prisoner of War # 3305
> Oflag 64
> Germany
>
> The Red Cross tells me that in sending cards to P.O.W. one should address the inside envelope fully & stamp (air mail) & then enclose in an outside envelope simply addressed–
> Prisoner of War Mail.
>
> The reason for the two envelopes is because Germany doesn't like any of our propaganda & the cancelling machine reads Buy War Bonds.

Sgt. Roland Moody, meanwhile, wrote on 19 March 1945 to describe a murderous assault on Della Torraccia, a mountain garrison in Italy—surprisingly, the censors didn't take out the place names. Metcalf replied with the news that Moody's colleague Charles Grace was in the first landing wave at Iwo Jima. To lighten the mood, he then adds that "We keep wishing you were back here and that we could put you to work supervising the straightening out of the stacks. They have got into very bad condition and we are going to have to make a special project when the war is over to read the shelves, inventory, catch up with back binding, etc."

By October 1945, Widener men were streaming back into the US. As soon as he was back in the States, Sgt. Moody wrote Metcalf to seek help securing early discharge to resume Widener work. In response, Metcalf swiftly drafted a letter to Moody's commanding officer, Lt. Col John H. Hay, Jr.:

> One of the members of your Battalion is a former member of the staff of the Harvard College Library, Roland H. Moody, who is in the Headquarters Company. While of course I do not want to do anything to interfere with regular Army arrangements, I

> am writing to say that Sgt Moody's services are very badly needed here in the Library at Harvard. During the War, we have had to let conditions in our main stack room run down becuse of lack of help. It was not a particularly serious matter because we did not have students doing research work. The close of the war has brought back a tremendous wave of men who are doing research work. . . . We are counting on Sgt Moody to take charge of this rehabilitation work, and . . . we should be very glad indeed to have him at the earliest possible moment.

Along the way, there were lighter intrusions of the outside world within the halls of Widener. In April 1939, Benny Goodman's publicist, Ira L. Steiner, offered the gift of a collection of the bandleader's recordings to the Harvard Theatre Collection, then housed in Widener. In his letter to Metcalf, Steiner wrote that "Benny Goodman, being not only the King of Swing but one of America's outstanding clarinetists, sees [the] American music is the music of today. He is preparing a complete repertory of early American songs, authentic melodies and rhythms of the fields and mountains, which he will introduce to the millions who follow wherever his clarinet leads." Steiner invited the library to join Goodman in this enterprise; Metcalf, alas, thought the connection too coarse and popular for the Harvard College Library, and declined. In 1984, as if in redress, Harvard would award Benny Goodman an honorary degree.

Widener attracted publicity of a different kind in May 1944, when Harry Elkins Widener's brother and sister gave the library a Gutenberg Bible. This complete copy on paper had been purchased in January 1912 by their grandfather, P.A.B. Widener, from the family's chief book dealer, A.S.W. Rosenbach of Philadelphia. This was not the first Gutenberg the Wideners had tried to purchase; they had previously been outbid by Henry Huntington, whose profligate spending drove up rare book prices on both sides of the Atlantic. P.A.B. had intended to give the Bible to Harry to serve as centerpiece for his own growing collection, but with Harry's death, the Bible remained in the family. The Widener Gutenberg was one of only seventeen paper copies in existence, four of which were in the United States.

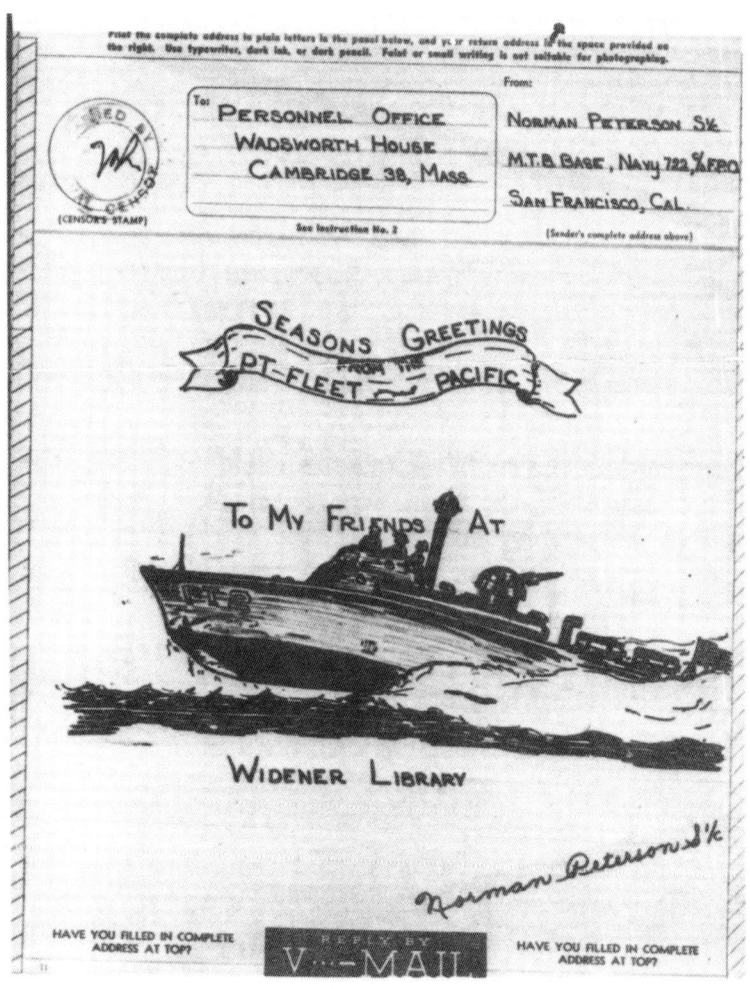

A picturesque note from a former Widener staff member Norman Peterson, who served in the Pacific during World War II, gave his old colleagues a glimpse of his new line of work.

IN THE MIDST OF THE WAR, METCALF PURSUED HIS AMBITIONS for Harvard's libraries. To fulfill his plans for off-site storage, he secured the cooperation of Boston area librarians, arranged funding, and contributed his inspirations to the design process. The resulting building, dubbed the New England Deposit Library (or NEDL for short), offered space for a million volumes and featured a reading room. Built in 1942, NEDL both suffered from and benefited from the exigencies of wartime; although steel intended for the stack was commandeered by the government for preparedness, the wood shelving built to replace it brought costs down considerably; the facility leased space to a government agency developing an aircraft camera, which needed its firmly-constructed floors to dampen vibrations during testing; the rental income helped the Depository pay off its mortgage in half the allotted time. But the government was not the Depository's only tenant: to attract government monies and tax subsidies, Metcalf had pursued the Depository as a collaborative venture; six Boston-area libraries joined Harvard, further defraying the cost. The building, according to Metcalf, came in below the $250,000 that Harvard had lent for its construction.

Another use of NEDL space was made by the Victory Book Campaign, which, like the A.L.A.'s World War I book project in Widener's basement, collected reading matter for distribution to service members. "Books collected by the Campaign were arranged by author," Metcalf later wrote, "and those regarded as suitable were turned over to Harvard; they included a large quantity of American fiction published after 1875. With minor exceptions, Harvard had collected little of this up to that time, but the English Department was now interested in it."

But NEDL was not designed for books in demand, but for the so-called "dead books" Eliot had described a half century before. In a library as diverse and active as Widener, however, "dead books" could be hard to find. Some of the bound newspapers were obvious candidates. Metcalf later wrote of this challenge in his memoirs.

> There was no need to keep the *New York Times* in Widener now that the Library had obtained a microfilm copy. We knew that some of the old files of Boston newspapers were rarely used, so these could be sent. One of the senior catalogers went through the Widener stack looking for multi-volume works of which the Library had many editions, few of them in demand. An example was Gibbon's *Decline and Fall of the Roman Empire*. If I remember correctly, there were more than sixty editions of this in Widener, including only a few that were of current interest. There were sets of old encyclopedias such as the *Britannica*, which needed to be preserved but were seldom used. There was a tremendous collec-

tion of primary, elementary, and secondary-school textbooks, which was not used heavily after the retirement of Dean Holmes of the Graduate School of Education.

"Altogether," Metcalf continued, "we found that nearly one-fifth of the bulk of the Widener collections could be sent to storage without causing very much inconvenience," and at a cost one-quarter of what it was to keep a book in the stacks (twenty-five cents versus one dollar). "Sometime in the late nineteen-forties," Metcalf continues, "a study was made of the number of calls for books that Harvard had sent to the Deposit Library, and we found that the average volume there was requested less than one percent as often as the average volume in the Widener stacks. Even so, many of the volumes in storage may well have been books held by no other American library, and we should have been unwilling to discard them."

Ultimately, NEDL would prove the least satisfactory of Metcalf's reforms. In library collections, obsolescence is self-fulfilling: the very marginality of the collections destined to be housed in NEDL led to their hasty recataloging, in which all books bound for storage received a call number from the same series, beginning with K. Thus, everything from education reform pamphlets to nineteenth-century historical works to superannuated encyclopedias was lumped together under one cataloging rubric, making them more difficult to winnow and search in the overflowing drawers of the card catalogs. Furthermore, despite NEDL's cost effectiveness, it had consumed much effort and attention, and yet it only offered Harvard space equivalent to about one-fifth the Widener stack.

For the time being, however, Metcalf's success with NEDL spurred the adoption of his plans in other areas, too. In the early forties, he had asked architects to draw up plans for a "Rare Books Annex" to occupy a hillock to the East of Widener, where Eliot had once wanted to build an octagonal addition to Gore Hall. These early drawings depicted a building attached to Widener by means of an ornate bridge big enough to accommodate offices and a reading room, complete with landscaping to tie the new building in with Widener. It soon became clear, however, that such an "annex" would violate the terms of the Widener gift. The project was saved, however, when Arthur Houghton stepped in. Harvard graduate, bibliophile, and architect *manqué*, Houghton had his own very specific ideas about what a rare books library should be; along with his money, he offered design ideas that helped differentiate the new institution from its parent. The newly minted Houghton Library opened in 1942, connected to Widener by a modest—and supposedly temporary—bridge, which would connect the rare books collection to its parent library until 2004.

The last of Metcalf's major initiatives was among the first for which he had laid plans. Nearly from the time of his arrival at Harvard, Metcalf had assiduously cultivated another potential donor, the financier Thomas Lamont. In Spring 1939, Lamont asked Metcalf about the library's needs over lunch at the Harvard Club in New York. Metcalf told him about a long-held dream of his to build a library specifically for undergraduates. When President Conant's report on college education, informally known as the *Red Book*, appeared in 1945, Lamont was inspired to write Metcalf. The *Red Book* charted a stirring course for American higher education in the postwar era: more meritocratic and achievement oriented than the genteel system of the past. "It is evident," Lamont wrote, "that if [the *Red Book*'s] recommendations are to be carried out successfully, the undergraduate library, which we have been talking about for a number of years, will be needed even more than it has been in the past." Though Lamont initially balked at the $1.5 million postwar price Metcalf estimated, he quickly changed his mind and made a gift of the entire amount.

But the end of the war brought a building boom to Harvard, and there was precious little space left in the Yard for new buildings. Undaunted, Metcalf suggested that the president himself make room for the new library.

> President Conant. . . . was living in the Dana-Palmer House on the site that I preferred. He did not want to move and did not like the suggestion. I said I believed that this was very much the best site. It was on the way between Harvard Yard, where the

> Freshman dormitories were, and the Freshman Union, where they took their meals; consequently it was an ideal place to catch them during their first years in college. The site was also between student classrooms and the houses where the other undergraduates lived. I very much wanted to have the library there. He was still unhappy, but said he would refer the matter to the Corporation, and I was given opportunities to talk informally with several of its members. The decision was to use the Yard site that I wanted.

Even James Bryant Conant, the President of Harvard, could be made to bend in the face of Keyes Dewitt Metcalf's big plans.

While Thomas Lamont furnished funds for the building, Metcalf needed to raise endowment money to pay operating costs. He began a public relations blitz, simultaneously seeking to attract alumni to donate money and to induce undergraduates to clamor for a library of their own. A flyer circulated; entitled "The Widener Reading Room, An Undergraduate view of it," it told of the woes the typical undergraduate faces when he tries to study in the big library. "Does anyone remember the old newsreel showing the melee on the floor of the New York Stock Exchange on a memorable day in 1929? If, out of some nostalgic urge, you would like to relive those exciting moneychanging moments, you might stop by the Widener Reading Room." The note goes on to diagnose the "ostentatious, uninviting" reading room's chief ills: "The pressing swirl of studious humanity in front of the delivery desk, the row on row of close-packed readers, the poor light, the sleep making atmosphere. . . . There is . . . a disturbed vastness about as conducive to study as the waiting room in the Grand Central Station." The hypothetical undergraduate is utterly rebuffed—his seat near a window taken, his ears buffeted by sounds bouncing off the arched ceiling, his books not available in any case. The note ends with an appeal to alumni, set in red type: "If you believe that the library is the heart of Harvard College, here is the perfect opportunity to express your belief."

In addition to this broadside, Metcalf published a newsletter, *The Open Shelf*, to convey news of the new library—and a sense of excitement—to students and donors. Lamont opened in 1949 on the former site of the President's house. The first Harvard building to embrace a modern architectural vocabulary unreservedly, Lamont Library immediately eased pressure on Widener to furnish books for undergraduates.

In Lamont Library, Metcalf, hoped, undergraduates would not merely find the books they needed for their classwork; they would learn the rudiments of scholarly research itself. To this end, and in marked contrast to Widener, Lamont Library's stacks were open. The collection was selected carefully to comprise both basic teaching materials and a diversity sufficient for research. Metcalf also hoped to instill a sense of undergraduate ownership of and entitlement to the library by limiting disciplinary oversight. "The supervision is at the doors," he wrote, "not elsewhere. Any book may be used freely anywhere within the building." Unfortunately, to make Lamont Library a zone free of strictures, Metcalf felt that it would need to be strictly off limits to women—a policy which would in time become symbolic of Harvard's stubborn conservatism in the face of women's rights.

By now, Metcalf had spent twelve years at Harvard, and the library had changed irrevocably. In the midst of the war, with staff and students in short supply and money for the University's

With its cool, elegant modernity, Lamont Library was designed to foster a sense of ownership and belonging in its student patrons.

Harvard's OPEN SHELF

Published in the interest of the LAMONT LIBRARY endowment by the Harvard Fund Council

JUNE, 1948   CAMBRIDGE, MASSACHUSETTS   VOL. I. NO. 1

THREE HARVARD BENEFACTORS

JOHN HARVARD
who gave a library, an estate, and a name.
(*An imaginary likeness by Daniel Chester French.*)

HARRY ELKINS WIDENER '07
memorialized by the library donated by his mother.

THOMAS W. LAMONT '92
whose many generous bequests included a $1,500,000 contribution toward building the new undergraduate library.

John Harvard's 400 Books
A GIFT THAT MULTIPLIED

IN 1638 John Harvard's modest library was undoubtedly one of the largest private collections in the American Colonies. Today its successor, the library of which it once formed the major part, is more than 10,000 times as large, requiring more than 140 miles of shelving.

Announcing
"Harvard's Open Shelf"
This is the first of several bulletins to be issued by the Harvard Fund Council to keep Harvard men informed as to the progress of the library endowment campaign; to call to their attention some of the interesting facts about the College Library, past and present; and to rekindle Harvard memories, associations, and traditions, which are part of the heritage of every Harvard alumnus.

Facts About the World's Largest University Library

Harvard University Library, with 5,000,000 volumes and pamphlets, is not only the largest university library in the world, but in the United States ranks second only to the Congressional Library in Washington.

There are more books in various Harvard libraries outside Widener than in the main collection. In all, there are 86 of these Special, Departmental, and House libraries.

Among the Library's outstanding collections are: Angling, Celtic, Chess, Cook Books, Folklore, Indic literatures, Italian Risorgimento, Law, the Mormons, Music, Ottoman Empire, Slavery, the Theatre (including a million playbills), and Tobacco.

Shortly before his premature death at the age of 30, the studious Charlestown preacher bequeathed his 400 volumes and one-half his personal fortune to the struggling young college that had been founded only two years before and had just convened its first classes.

So grateful was the Colony for this generous bequest that the General

Thomas W. Nason, N.A.
Ex Libris: JOHN HARVARD
The only volume from John Harvard's library definitely known to have survived the burning of old Harvard Hall in 1764 is this copy of John Downame's *Christian Warfare Against the Deuill, World and Flesh*. Fortunately, it had been loaned to a student named Briggs some four months before the fire and Mr. Briggs had been a trifle slow in returning it.

Court ordered "that the colledge agreed upon formerly to bee built at Cambridg shalbee called Harvard Colledge."

Nearly three-fourths of John Harvard's books were theological treatises,

Harvard's Open Shelf was one of Metcalf's canny attempts at promoting Lamont Library to the Harvard community.

civilian efforts hard to find, Metcalf had relentlessly pursued a program of growth as ambitious as any since the Coolidge era was built. In that time, Metcalf had become a leader of the library profession, and his influence now extended far beyond the new buildings in the Yard. After the war, he proposed a new collaborative acquisitions scheme for American academic libraries. Dubbed the Farmington Plan, it was an attempt to fill the gap in European acquisitions caused by many years of war; at the same time, it took advantage of America's new global reach and responsibility throughout the world to internationalize collections. Like Harvard at large, Metcalf's library was vast, energetic, and ineluctably complex. And now, with his sleek new undergraduate library, with NEDL holding overflow collections in check, and with Houghton Library flourishing under an inspired staff of scholar-librarians, Metcalf turned his attention to Widener itself.

In Lamont Library's modern Forum Room, Metcalf convened a meeting of his colleagues from academic libraries across the country.

"Harvard's departmental libraries," he told them, "are now larger than the central unit and are growing more rapidly. Without a more centralized administration . . . this growth of the peripheral units will be hard to keep within bounds." Recognizing the increasingly complex demands placed on the administrators of the library, Metcalf calls for a new class of librarians trained not as catalogers or reference specialists, but as administrators. While he admits that the library schools aren't producing such candidates, neither does he "believe that shifting a professor into the librarian's office will solve the problem." Instead, Metcalf calls for fellowships for "young persons of the highest caliber," who would spend two to three years in a melange of business, public administration, and bibliography classes, with an internship year supplemented by a course in library administration modelled on the Harvard Business School's case system. Such a program would in time produce the kind of leaders the newly professionalized, bureaucratic library needs–leaders uncannily like Keyes Dewitt Metcalf.

Of course, no university in America was willing to give out "large fellowships" to attract "young people of the highest caliber" into librarianship. Not long after Metcalf's tenure ended, Harvard would seek to appease faculty concerns about the University's enormous library by shifting a professor into the librarian's office. And yet, here as elsewhere, Metcalf was prescient enough: the profession of librarianship would turn in the direction of administrative professionalism, away from the model of the scholar-librarian exemplified by the likes of Justin Winsor, T. Frank Currier, and William Coolidge Lane.

Metcalf and other leaders made their impact on the library felt, but the character of daily life in the library was determined by other, less illustrious figures. Perhaps chief among such characters was John Shea, superintendent of Widener's stacks and physical plant and the professional and spiritual successor to Frank Carney. Shea had begun his Harvard career under Carney; near the end of his career, he would say that Carney "had practically brought [him] up." Similarities between the two men were striking: like Carney, Shea was the son of an Irish immigrant and single parent; like Carney, he liked school, but gave it up to seek work; like Carney, his introduction to Harvard came through the laundry he delivered to professors. Shea started in 1905 as a coatroom attendant in Gore Hall, but quickly moved into the stack. He was in the Widener coatroom in 1927, however, to turn away a student who tried to bring a bottle of ink into the library.

That student complained to Coolidge; and he would not be the last to object to Shea's coarse ways. "Possibly you may be aware of the conduct . . . of one of your assistants," wrote a "Disgusted Student" in 1940; "namely one John Shea—in regards to young ladies under his supervision":

> This man, judging by his conduct, is not fit for the position he holds. His ignorant, arrogant, and I might say beastly boorish attitude towards these young ladies does not quite fit into the surroundings of Widener Library. I think people today have a hard enough time as it is, without being insulted, abused, embarrassed and humiliated in the presence of we students. I have witnessed these outbursts many times.

> People suffer from "inferiority complex"—John Shea's malady, diagnosed correctly:—"superiority complex", caused by an overdose of mental stagnation.—A dull, slow-witted, ignorant hypocritical character, holding a position in the manner described, does not speak well of Wideners fame. Do we students have to endure this specimen of subnormality?
>
> There should be some solution!

But if students and coworkers objected to the brusque Shea, faculty and administrators appreciated him. Metcalf, who sent Shea postcards from his vacations, responded mildly to this letter, noting that he had merely asked Shea "not to do his rebuking in public." Metcalf relied on Shea to manage the often-tricky class relations that still obtained among faculty, professional staff, and laborers. In a memo to Shea he reminds him that

> from time to time trouble results when stack attendants use the stack elevators when they are wanted by officers of the Univ. Please ask Mr. Moody to tell the boys:
>
> 1) That they must always use the utmost courtesy when there is a conflict of needs.
>
> 2) That they should not use the elevators when they are going up only one flight or down one or two flights unless of course they are taking a book truck with them.
>
> 3) That officers of the University always have the right of way unless the boys actually have a book truck in the elevator. On such occassions they should take the elevator to the station to which they are going and get the book truck out as rapidly as possible.

On another occasion, Metcalf asks Shea to tell a group of janitors not to wait outside the library while waiting for their pay; he found their presence unsightly.

Metcalf was not the only superior who relied on Shea. Arthur Schlesinger, Jr., wrote Shea personally in 1950:

> Dear John, Is there any chance of getting my study (Widener 195) painted this summer? Judging from appearances, it has

not been painted since the McKinley administration; and it is undoubtedly the drabbest and dreariest office in the entire library. Any reasonably light color would do. I would be everlastingly grateful if something could be done.

Don't have too strenuous a summer!

Long before Schlesinger called upon Shea to paint his study, the stack superintendent had earned a reputation as an autodidact and savant of the stacks. Like his predecessor Frank Carney, Shea used his decades among Widener's books as a kind of extended college education. Though never as learned as Carney, Shea knew the collections as well as anyone ever did. In 1937, he was featured in a *Boston Herald* profile by Peggy Lamson under the headline, "Could You Keep Track, Mentally, of More Than a Million Books?" Lamson opined that "if one were hunting for a combination of first class sleuth and a modern memory expert the person to look up would be John Shea, superintendent of the book stacks at the Harvard College Library . . . . There are 1,007,000 [sic] and some odd hundred books in the Harvard library, and it is not an exaggeration to say that John Shea knows where every one of them is." According to Lamson, Shea knew the topics studied by all of the 400 or so holders of studies and carrels, so he knew where to look first for mislaid books. He knew which French books are usually on reserve, and which Widener holdings are duplicated elsewhere. " . . . [T]hough not a scholar himself, he knows books so well that he is able to judge by titles alone into what special fields of research they belong." In closing, Lamson describes how important Shea is to all aspects of life in the library. "So it is of small wonder that every one connected in any way with the library smiles fondly at the mention of his name and says, 'Oh, John Shea—I can't imagine this library without him. There's nothing he can't or doesn't do to make things run smoothly. He's everywhere at once.'" According to Lamson, Shea periodically checked his daily progress with a pedometer, and found that he walked up to eight miles a day in the stacks.

Along with his faultless memory and his indefatigability, Shea was remembered by his colleagues for his oral idiosyncrasies and

John Shea

infelicities. He salted his speech with malapropisms. In pursuit of a lost book, he told a colleague, he would "leave no stone unthrown." I hope he had learned to do his rebuking in private by the time he admonished an assistant who was, he said, "getting very laxative in your work."

After forty-eight years of service, John Shea knew the locations of 2,200,000 books—the fruit of a considerable postgraduate education for a man who never finished grammar school. Harvard understood, awarding Shea an honorary MA upon his retirement in 1953.

Shea was probably the last Widener staff member to have worked in Gore Hall. He had helped with Carney's monumental transfers of books out of the old library and into the new; he saw the great library rise in the Yard; he watched students and staff leave to fight two world wars, and watched them return to change Harvard and the country.

For Metcalf, too, much had changed. In his effort to turn Widener into a "research center," he had changed the character of the building dramatically. With rare books, undergraduate reserves, and many special collections gone, Widener was now a library for the humanities and social sciences; accordingly, its status as hub of intellectual life at Harvard had diminished. It had become instead the administrative center of a burgeoning Harvard College Library system. In an extensive renovation of lighting in the building, Metcalf had ordered the installation of up-to-date fluorescent fixtures; ornate ceilings were hidden behind acoustic tile and rococo surfaces were painted white for maximum reflectivity.

There were more fundamental problems as well. In the push for space and ever-greater acquisitions, the Widener stack had slipped out of control. John Shea's prodigious memory and book-hunting intuition could not supply the needs of all the scholars searching for lost books, and even the most adept scholars found Widener's shelves increasingly alienating. The eminent historian Howard Mumford Jones wrote Associate Librarian Ralph Haynes in 1950 to regale him with a lost-in-the-stacks story:

> Tomorrow morning at nine o'clock I am to lecture on the poetry of Robert Frost. I wished this morning to revise my lecture notes and to consult a variety of opinion concerning him. I therefore went to my study; and since my own copy of the Literary History of the United States was at home, I began by trying to consult some of the numerous copies in the Widener. I went first to the card catalogue on Floor Four; and got there two numbers. I then went to stacks only to find that the bibiliographical volume (III) was not there. I retraced my steps to the Reading Room and after some search, found my book, out of which I copied a series of about twelve references I wished to consult . . . .

After listing the wanted titles, which including Lawrance Roger Thompson's 1942 study of Robert Frost, *Fire and Ice*, Jones continues to relate his travails:

> I went to look up the number of the Thompson book, and found that there was no copy in the Widener Library. I filled out an order card, and took it to the order department, where one of the staff said "Let's look in the Union Catalogue." We did[;] there were (and are) copies in the Poetry Room and in Lamont, but none in the Widener Library. Thompson's book is a standard work on one of the greatest American poets, and I said I could not understand why, under the rule which keeps copies of such work, or rather one copy of such a work, in the Widener,

all the copies (two) had been lodged in Lamont. I went to Mr. Metcalf's office, and made a rather vigorous complaint. This locomotion occupied a good deal of space and time. I may add that the book was requested from Lamont, the messenger sought to deliver it in Study 117, and was prevented only by the intervention of Professor Sherburn, who sent him to my study....

Jones then seeks another volume, which he discovers misplaced on the stack shelves. Next, he starts the hunt for the journals:

> *The American Scholar* is shelved on Floor A; the *New England Quarterly* under New England; the *Classical Journal* is shelved on floor 5; and *College English* is in Educ on Floor B. I shall not go into the matter of distribution East, South, and West of these periodicals, but it is evident that merely traveling around the stacks after them takes up time....

He discusses further troubles finding the sought-after articles before concluding:

> Now let us grant certain things. It is nobody's fault that periodicals containing articles about Frost should be scattered from floor 5 to floor B, but when, after climbing around, waiting for elevators, going back to check numbers or to discover whether a bound periodical is charged out, lost, or mislaid, most of one's morning has disappeared, one does become exasperated. Moreover, I cannot see why is is assumed that a special library about poetry is to be sequestered in Lamont, so that no Radcliffe student can get at it, and that a professor, to get at it, must climb out of Widener, climb up at Lamont, find the book, and then return with it or without it as the case may be, when his study is put into Widener with the express purpose of keeping books close to him. I do not see why the fullest biographical account of the most important American poet is kept for Lamont students, and no copy left in Widener. If it be argued that it is a simple thing to send for such a book, I must point out that: (a) who is to send for it? (b) the book being sent for is not necessarily going to be found under the open stack system; (c) I was under the impression that one copy of works of this character was to be kept in Widener. If one works, as I do, at a typewriter, once cannot drag his typewriter into Lamont.

> As for the periodical problem, I should heartily favor a rule that did not permit the charging out of scholarly and professional periodicals.
>
> Doubtless any one step in the process I have described is defensible in library terms, and therefore they are all defensible, and I can clearly be proved to be wrong. But the net result of the presumed advantage of having a free access to the stacks of this great collection, with the additional advantage of a study in the building, is that my working morning was wasted—and I am, I suppose, a rather expensive fellow for Harvard to support.

Mumford's last comment is illuminating. As Metcalf had transformed the library, he had transformed its readers as well. By giving them greater access and freedom of mobility in the stacks, by placing the onus for finding books on their shoulders, he had turned them, essentially, into stack pages. And for those who lacked John Shea's intimacy with the vagaries of the stack, the prospect was a daunting one.

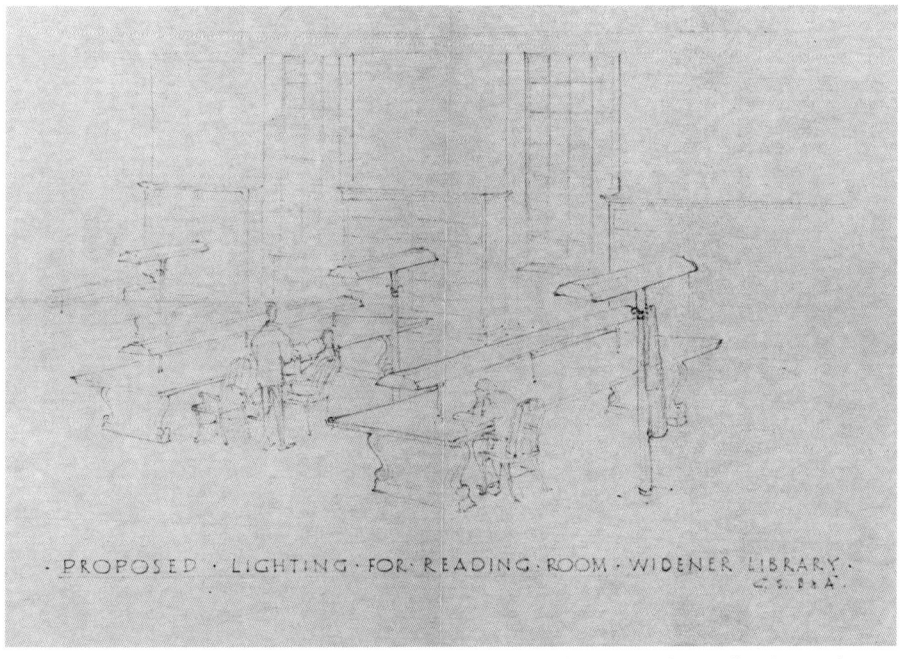

Not all of Metcalf's changes were made. This proposed lighting scheme for the Widener reading room would have dramatically altered the character of the space.

Metcalf's changes, meanwhile, continued. In the early fifties he altered Widener with subtle yet comprehensive renovations, installing fluorescent lighting throughout the public areas of the building, installing copper roofing over skylights in the Reading Room, and modernizing elevators. Faculty were consulted, but they were concerned with little beyond the furnishing of more studies. Their insistence on this point was so great that Metcalf considered adding a mezzanine in the Reading Room, which would have offered extra shelving and space for twenty-five small

A glimpse into Widener's massive card catalog in the nineteen-fifties.

studies. Ultimately, the cost for this last feature was found to be too great; the tab for Metcalf's new lighting, new ceilings, and elevator rehabilitation in 1950-51 was over $250,000.

In 1952, Metcalf proposed a merger of Widener's two catalogues, the Union and the Public Catalogues. The first held cards for all Harvard-owned books but lacked subject cards and cross-references; the second listed only the books of the Harvard College Library and was cross-referenced extensively. While the system had its merits—in a large and busy library, staff and readers vied for access to catalogue records—the bicameral system had longed perplexed student and faculty alike. In proposing the merger, Metcalf emphasized increased convenience to faculty, especially those without studies in Widener; he pointed out that the change would save some $14,000 a year in duplicate cataloguing costs, would increase access to the collections for those who don't use the first floor catalogue, and would free up needed space. But for many on the faculty, Metcalf had proposed one change too many. Howard Mumford Jones spoke up once more, and this time for many colleagues, when he sent Metcalf this 1950 memorandum:

> After long hesitating, I have decided to write you about the library.... I for one would would much prefer postponing [costly] changes of this sort [catalogue consolidation, structural change], which clearly do not have any great weight of faculty opinion behind them, in order that the money could be used to increase wages and salaries, however mildly, among the library staff and employees. I must honestly say that there has seemed to me to be a descending curve of morale in the staff over the last few years....I have now learned to resign myself to the experience that, out of a list of a dozen titles I wish to consult in American history and literature, at least two or three will be missing, lost, misplaced, or otherwise untraceable.... [R]elations between the Lamont Library on the one hand, and the books in Widener... remain so mysterious that I have simply ceased to waste my time and energy trying to get a book on reserve for my own course. It is this perpetual kind of petty annoyance, this constant frittering away of one's own energies, this wasting of steps as one goes hither and yon trying to locate a book that, I think, annoys not only me but a good many other members of the faculty primarily concerned with books.... In

sum, what I am saying, with some pain in my heart, is that the library difficulties, from where I sit, seem to me to be personnel and professional rather than architectural.

In the end, the President and Fellows chose not to authorize the merger of the catalogues. In a June 1952 letter to Conant, Metcalf strove (none too successfully) to give a positive cast to his disappointment, describing the eventual necessity of the changes he proposed. He notes that the origin of the dual catalogue was an artifact of Widener: "The Widener building was the first great modern monumental library building that made necessary by its architectural arrangement two catalogues instead of one. As is often the case, other universities followed our example, and the two catalogue system grew up throughout the country. Here was an opportunity to change what seems to me an unnecessarily expensive pattern."

Metcalf concludes with a mournful coda to the great changes he had stirred in Widener:

> My final point is one that I am not sure is a proper one for me to make, but I do want to call attention to the belief which comes as a result of forty years of administrative experience in libraries, that any change made in a library results in criticism, and that much of the criticism of the merger proposal comes from a cumulating feeling that Keyes Metcalf was always changing things. Houghton, Lamont, and the New England Deposit Library irritated a good many members of the Faculty. But changes ordinarily are accepted once they have been accomplished, and I believe that if, ten years from now, the merger is carred out, it will be generally accepted and will be welcomed as Lamont, Houghton, and the New England Deposit Library have been.

Metcalf retired in 1954. His ambitions had defined a course for Widener–indeed all of Harvard's libraries–for the next fifty years. And yet the library was in turmoil. President Nathan Pusey's Provost, McGeorge Bundy, called Metcalf's final annual report "one long wail." Far from seeking out a young library administrator of the highest caliber, central administration moved to place the library more firmly under its own control.

Metcalf was succeeded by former provost Paul Buck in the role of College Librarian; Douglas Bryant, who had served under Metcalf for many years, became University Librarian. Never again would control of the University and College Libraries rest in one officer's hands, and Bryant and Buck both understood that the final arbiter of decisions about the library's future would be neither of them, but the Faculty Library Committee instead.

BY 1953, CONANT WAS TIRED AS WELL. UNDER HIS LEADERSHIP, the university had become deeply involved in the politics of American power. Harvard scholars had consulted at high levels in the Roosevelt and Truman administrations; Harvard scientists conducted research on war-related technologies; Conant himself had administered the program that built and tested the first Atomic bomb. In the wake of American victory and the runup to the Cold War, Harvard served as a symbol both of American values—George Marshall took the occasion of his honorary degree at the 1947 Commencement to unveil plans for the economic revitalization of Europe—and of the kind of intellectual power Thorstein Veblen had predicted would belong to America in the twentieth century.

Despite such service, Harvard's preeminence bred resentment, which in the early years of the Cold War was expressed in terms of the struggle against Communism. Dwight D. Eisenhower—who had earned an honorary degree himself in 1946—railed against the "Harvard words" in which his foes expressed themselves in the 1950 presidential campaign. Senator Joseph McCarthy turned his ire on Harvard, too, calling it a nest of Communist sympathizers. Boston redbaiters also trained their sights on Harvard. In 1952, the *Boston Post* editor John Fox began a crusade against libraries, pointing out that a host of local institutions carried Communist books and periodicals; Widener, with its extensive research collections, was singled out for special abuse.

HARVARD'S LIBRARY HAS COMMUNIST NEWSPAPERS

Communist newspapers devoted to the destruction of democracy and imported straight from Moscow are available for all who wish them at Harvard's Widener Library. Twenty-nine Kremlin-published newspapers are available and offered free of charge.

Topping the list of Russian papers on the shelves of the library are Moscow-published and Cominform directed newspapers *Izvestia* and *Pravda*.

There's nothing to stop impressionable high school and college students from reading the four propaganda periodicals that appear in English at the library. In every issue American patriots become the target of the vicious communist propaganda.

Thousands of Moscow-published books also appear in the Harvard Library's listings purchased by money given to educate the youth of America. On none of the listing cards is any mention made of the fact that these books are printed under the dictates of the communist regime in Russia to warn student readers.

Russian literature is up-to-date and much can be obtained in English as well as in Russian.

Communists can use the Harvard Library's reading rooms side by side with Harvard College students. Material that might ordinarily be hard for the communist to obtain because of the importation restrictions is offered on a silver dish to any Red propagandist.

There is nothing to stop the communists from teaching and reading the contents of both the Russian and the English editions of the Moscow supervised literature to college students who come to the reading rooms to study.

For a brief time, the Boston libraries were in the spotlight. A committee looked into the Post's allegations on behalf of the trustees of the Boston Public Library. But the institutions stood fast: Harvard declined to respond, and the trustees of the Boston Public Library declined to remove the books in question.

Conant abruptly left Harvard in 1953 to become High Commissioner to occupied Germany. Incoming Harvard President Nathan Marsh Pusey appeared on television, using the new medium to combat McCarthy's allegations and raise the public profile of the Harvard presidency at once.

Harvard was buffeted by changes not merely ideological, but also cultural in scope. After the war, an influx of new students more mature and independent-minded than previous generations expected unheard-of freedoms in pursuit of their education. Student culture was changing in ways that a tradition-bound university found hard to assimilate, and in Widener the pangs were felt as deeply as anywhere else. By the mid-1950's, Metcalf's successor, Douglas Bryant, acquiesced to the concerns of faculty and staff by forming a "Decorum Committee" to deal with a perceived breakdown of order in the library. In accepting a request to serve on the committee in 1958, Associate Librarian Ralph Haynes offered Bryant his suggestions:

> We should have, I think, a sort of floorwalker who combines the duties of an adviser, with that of a custodian in keeping order. On the helpful side, he could direct people who are looking for the Reference Desk, Circulation Desk, Periodical Room, the Archives, the Map Room or even for myself. . . . [H]e could keep his eye out for those who appear to be lost (and there are more such than one might think), find out what they want, and set them on the right road. . . .
>
> On the side of order, he would stop smoking where it is not permitted, and also lounging. I for one, if we had such a person on duty, would have no smoking in the foyer on the upper level, nor on the stairways, nor in the public catalogue, and I would permit no sitting or extended loafing in the foyer, on the stairs, or on the windowsills—and no sliding down the bannister from the stair landing.

In a subsequent report, the committee strove to downplay the seriousness of problems of order and discipline in the library.

> One is tempted to say that the age old cry "O tempora, o mores" was never more apt than it is today; but a little reflection will indicate that this is not so. We have come a long way since the time a century ago when tobacco juice on the floors of Gore Hall was a major problem. Rather we are in a mild recession in the field of manners, perhaps a postwar phase.

Discussing problems ranging from smoking to "lounging and loitering" to the shocking prospect of students' feet propped on tables, the Committee was sanguine, though it did recommend the hiring of an security officer to enforce regulations (and stipulated that the "hazardous practice" of smoking in the stacks be treated as a serious offence). But critics of the new licentiousness were not mollified. In January 1960, President Pusey received a letter from Ernest Villas of the *Hellenic Chronicle*, a newspaper that served Boston's Greek community.

> Recently I had the pleasure of visiting beautiful and impressive Widener Library for the first time. It is truly a magnificent tribute to man's constant search for knowledge and truth, and an edifice of which Harvard University must be very proud.
>
> While in the Library, however, I noticed something that completely appalled me. I was deeply disappointed to note that students are allowed to smoke, albeit in certain sections, of the Library proper. It was even further disappointing to note the condoning of behavior which allows students' feet propped up on library tables....
>
> I am sincerely and deeply concerned about these things, Dr. Pusey, for from such seemingly minor items is the downfall of nations created.

Neither Villas nor Pusey knew how fractured Harvard—and the nation—would be by decade's end. A 1963 memorandum regarding "Conditions in the Widener Reading Room" indexes the social changes manifesting themselves in Widener and throughout the university:

There is a substantial amount of dissatisfaction with conditions in the Widener Reading Room. First of all, the tables are often too crowded; there are times when it is hard to find a place to sit down. Secondly, there is a feeling that use of the room to such a large extent as no more than a study hall impairs its higher level use as a place to do serious work with a good collection of reference books at hand. Thirdly, there is a feeling that the general atmosphere of the room is too informal and undignified.

Overcrowding could be reduced somewhat if some acceptable way could be found to exclude students from nearby colleges. At present, a sign at the door reading "Open only to members of the Harvard and Radcliffe Colleges and others who have been granted library privileges" is the only direct deterrent. This stops the conscientous type person whom we might be willing to have as a guest and is ignored by the less desirable elements among the visitors....

Overcrowding is only a part of the problem. There is frequent complaint as to the informal, undignified appearance of those in the room. To some extent, the objections are to specific acts which may be banned. The present ban against food and drink is well enforced, and without great difficulty. There is a rule against putting feet on tables (or, more common and slightly less crass, putting legs across the corner of a table), but this has gotten out of hand so far as enforcement by the professional staff is concerned.... From time to time it is necessary to speak to someone who sinks well below even the very low community standard of dress, for instance a man with his shirt front completely open. However, the hard fact remains that a great deal of the criticism of the reading room is simply criticism of the standards of dress of the student community. Students do not dress worse in Widener than they do in other places, though their dress may appear more out of place in a monumental reading room than it does elsewhere.

It also seems apparent that some of the criticism of the conditions in the Widener Reading Room comes from those who simply do not like to see boys and girls studying together. It is probably true that the coeducational nature of the reading room is one of the two factors that give it a substantially higher noise level than prevails in the Lamont reading areas,

> the other being the presence of the Reference Desk. However, the noise situation is largely self policing. When talking disturbs other students, they usually make their disapproval effectively felt. Allegations that necking goes on openly in the reading room are exaggerated.
>
> A final topic to be considered is smoking. At present, smoking is allowed in the large central section and the east end, or in other words all that portion of the room in which reference books are shelved. It is not allowed in the west end, which is a part of the Periodical Room. There have been some requests to enlarge the non-smoking area....
>
> In conclusion it seems that much of the dissatisfaction with the Widener Reading Room is really dissatisfaction with the present community standards....

More momentous changes were on the horizon, of which feet on tables were but an uncertain harbinger. Students for a Democratic Society, or SDS, was formed in Michigan in 1962. By 1969 its Harvard chapter, led by future progressive leaders Tom Hayden and Todd Gitlin, had become the most vocal student group on campus, protesting everything from Harvard's curriculum to the presence of the ROTC on campus to the university's alleged implication in the escalating war in Vietnam. During a visit to a Quincy House seminar in 1966, Secretary of Defense Robert McNamara was mobbed by students, forced to escape from an angry crowd through one of Harvard's fabled steam tunnels. The following year, protesters held a recruiter from Napalm manufacturer Dow Chemical hostage for seven hours. Radical students teamed up with sympathetic faculty in the Department of Social Relations to offer a series of disestablishmentarian courses; by 1969, Soc Rel 149, "Radical Perspectives on Social Change," boasted 900 students.

Discord reached its peak in the Spring of 1969, when SDS activists and sympathizers took over University Hall, the home of the university's central administration. Their demands included the ejection of the ROTC from campus and an end to Harvard's "colonial" expansion in Cambridge and Boston. Unwilling to bend to students and concerned about sensitive university records falling into unfriendly hands, President Pusey called in the police. At 5 AM, police from surrounding communities converged on the Yard. In an assault lasting barely twenty minutes they cleared the building of protesters, injuring about fifty of them in the process.

Staff, students, and faculty were appalled, both by the insubordinate student uprising and its violent end at the hands of the police. On April 17, 1969, Widener staff circulated a petition which, in its condemnation of the students' actions and the administration's response, highlights both the tension and the confusion of the time:

> I. We the undersigned employees of the Harvard College Library are in sympathy with the rest of the community in suspending activities on Friday, Saturday, Monday, and Tuesday morning for the purpose of giving full attention to the issues raised by recent events in the University.
>
> II. We feel that the occupation of University Hall and the eviction of the Deans was unacceptable.
>
> III. We repudiate the decision by administration to call in the police Thursday morning, the lack of consultation between student and faculty representatives, and the resort to violence by the police.
>
> IV. Interpretation of this is the province of each individual staff member.

While faculty agonized over what discipline to mete out, students and many staff convened a strike in protest of the administration's forceful dealings with the students. In Widener, meanwhile, a small cadre of faculty and librarians patrolled the halls, ostensibly to defend the building against incursions by radical students.

Their fears were not entirely unreasonable. University libraries had been damaged in student actions across the country; more disturbingly, Widener itself had been the focus of an attack which, while certainly unconnected to ideology and protest, reflected the anarchic tensions of the times. On 19 August 1969, a young man named Vito Aras climbed from the stacks to the roof of Widener, lowered himself into one of the light courts, and broke into the Widener Memorial Rooms, intent on stealing the Gutenberg Bible from the prominent vitrine in which it resided. Reporters were captivated by the psychedelic romance of Aras's act, referring to him as a "human fly," and also as a "mystic" who "dated a witch" and wore an amulet to protect himself from evil magic. Wire service reports claimed he was the son of an organist and a librarian. For all this, his plan was well-conceived: Aras had hidden in a top-floor restroom until the library closed. But while trying to climb out with his prize, he fell. Some reporters called him "brilliant," painting through his story a picture of a troubled sixties-era youth.

News of the theft was picked up by wire services and ran in papers around the country. Many papers included a UPI photo which showed, from above, the wall of the light court with the Memorial Room's bay window, with a dotted line showing the path of the burglar from the roof to the window, from the window to the ground, with a boxed X to mark his landing. This coverage induced a fresh flurry of letters to Harvard curators to consult about family Bibles or the theft of books. Letters came in from Old Lyme, Connecticut, Union City, California, and Macon, Georgia, asking for appraisals and advice on Bibles, most of which dated from the nineteenth century. H. K. Jarrett, for instance, wrote on Jarrett Paint & Glass Company stationery, 27 September 1969, addressing himself to "Harvard Library":

> Several weeks ago there was an article in our local newspaper regarding a Gutenburg bible which had some sort of mishap in your library . . . .I think that I have one of these bibles.
>
> I am sending to you copies of the front and back of the fly leaf, also a picture of the bible. The first half of the book was printed in 1739 and the second half in 1742.

> It has been in my family a long time. I am seventy two years old and my father inherited this bible from his family before I was born. It is in good condition . . . .
>
> If I have something worth while I would certainly like to know it and I considered you as the best possible source of information. It could easily be something which should be preserved for posterity and then someone might want it worse than I do.

Mrs. C. H. Castle of Grand Rapids, Michigan, wrote not about a Gutenberg Bible, but about a statue of its printer:

> For many years I have had in my possession, a replica in heavy metal of the famous Mr Gutenberg. The statue is beautifully detailed in every way. It shows him standing on one of the presses with an open bible in his hand. The features of his face, hands, etc. always get the second look from friends.
>
> My purpose for writing is to find out if this statue has any significant monetary value as far as the association with the bible is concerned. I wouldn't fret for long, if I did part with it for a satisfactory amount of money.

Roger E. Stoddard of Houghton Library replied to Mrs. Castle, telling her that her statue "would not be of interest to the Harvard Library. I have seen statuettes like yours on many occasions in antique shops. There is obviously a market for them but the price tags I have seen have always been quite modest."

Despite the impertinences of students and the depredations of the police, Harvard and its libraries continued to hold meaning, however confused and inchoate, for the country at large. At the library, meanwhile, fear remained high. In meetings on security matters in 1969, library administrators discussed the possibility of a student takeover of some or all of Widener, as well as the prospect of a violent attack on collections or staff; someone suggested hiring armed guards to patrol the Widener stacks. Roger Stoddard of Houghton Library remembers that he and other younger members of the College Library's administrative staff were shocked at this, reminding their senior colleagues of the damage that would be done to student relations, not to mention Harvard's reputation, were officers to so much as draw their weapons on protesters.

In retrospect, the antics of Vito Aras seem removed from the high-minded highjinks of student activists, which in the event were never focussed on the library. But to some on the faculty, the protesters' actions seemed little different from the acts of criminals or, worse, demagogues. There were students, it seemed, willing to tear down everything connected with the traditions of higher education—and what more apt symbol of those traditions than the library? The dangers were especially apparent to European faculty members old enough to have seen the rise of fascism, which for many of them had first appeared in the form of student rallies and book-bonfires on the campuses of German universities. But the library, like the canonical bodies of knowledge it could not help representing, had diminished in the minds of students as a symbol of the university's power and prestige, except in its most minimal and automatic functions. There is an irony here, of course: for Widener had from the start accommodated the old and the new—veneration of the canon and restless experiment, the rituals of the temple and the labors of the laboratory. But in their own revolutionary stirrings, the students of the sixties had recast this age-old conflict in new terms. Not only the value of different kinds of knowledge, but the method of its administration, was now up for grabs. In retrospect, this may be seen as a clear reaction against the administrative approach to knowledge envisioned by Veblen and put into practice by Conant and his generation. Against a model of knowledge that privileged the pragmatic and the "useful" over the good and the beautiful—necessitating a strict regime controlling its ascent into usefulness—the revolution in American education in the nineteen-fifties and sixties sought to free knowledge from all governing restrictions or standards, be they historical, critical, aesthetic, or administrative in nature. In the end, they misunderstood the radical nature of the SDS vision, in which Widener was not so much symbolic of hegemony as it was irrelevant to the structure of power in the University.

ULTIMATELY, WIDENER EMERGED UNSCATHED, SAFELY REMOVED as it was from the most violent and fractious events of the nineteen-sixties. Yet at the same time, Widener underwent changes that would in the long run prove more radical than the SDS agenda.

Widener's vast store of books both necessitated and impeded automation. Librarians at Harvard had long been searching for ways to automate the vast amounts of information work that go on in a library so large. Through the forties, a pneumatic tube was used to send call slips into the stack. In 1955, staff member Garry Hall delivered a remarkable proposal for a Rube-Goldberg proto-computer system using "magnetic memory equipment with random access." His report describes a system worthy of the pulp science fiction of the period: Borrowers would be furnished with blank call slips, which they would insert into a terminal with a keyboard. "As the borrower types," Hall writes, "the call number . . .is being typed on 11 machines, one on each level of the stacks, and one at the counter, and it is simultaneously interrogating the magnetic memory that is storing the record of charged out books." The system's "magnetic memory" checks records to find whether the book is available, and "[t]his information is also recorded on the ten machines in the stacks and the one at the counter. . . . . In addition to typing the call number, the machine used by the borrower is also punching a code into the edge of the card. This represents the call number of the book." After books are paged in the stacks, their punched-and-typed cards are placed on an opaque projector at the delivery desk so the "man" who requested the book will see that it is available for pickup. The screen is tabular, so that each image is thrown onto a numbered zone; the patron asks for the book by number. Another machine then reads from the card the type of loan indicated for the book, and places on a "magnetic belt" a code letter to indicate due date, call number, and other data. When the book is returned, its card is fed through a machine that erases the loan record from the belt; as a result, the belt only holds information regarding outstanding loans for the generation of overdue notices. Hall concludes by envisioning Widener hooked up by "cable" to other libraries, allowing "machines located in other libraries to interrogate the memory unit."

Hall's concept, while fanciful, strove to meet real needs. The university library by the late sixties was adding two hundred thousand volumes a year; Widener alone grew by some fifty thousand books annually. Such growth had long fueled experimentation at Harvard; circulation had been automated in 1938, when General Assistant Fred Kilgour (who would later develop the computerized catalog database known as OCLC) adapted a card-sorting system, in which cards perforated according to date were winnowed by means of a knitting-needle-like stylus. Meanwhile, the pursuit of technology, in such forms as the then-experimental Machine-Readable Catalog (MARC) records and computerized systems for cataloging, acquisitions, and circulation, which would seemingly burst on the scene with world-changing force two decades later, were already undergoing testing in Widener.

By 1963, the library was keeping track of loans with an IBM 1401 computer. The size of an upright piano, and with a suite of peripherals–punch card reader, input terminal, magnetic tape recorder, and jukebox-sized disk drive–the 1401 filled a small room. It was programmed in a fiendishly difficult language called Autocoder, and communicating with it was painful; commands had to be encoded on punchcards, which were fed through the reader to record the data on magnetic tape, which only then could be read and processed by the computer. And with its rental price of $2,500 a month, librarians had to key many boxes of cards to make it worth the price. And yet the IBM 1401 was the first truly practical computer for non-science applications. Widener's 1401, painstakingly programmed by Associate Librarian Foster Palmer, was used to convert Harvard's manuscript shelflists to computer records, which were then printed as bound catalogs of Harvard's collection and sold on a subscription basis to hundreds of libraries. The project was conceived by Richard De Gennaro, who would later serve as Librarian of Harvard College for the debut of Harvard's online catalog and the conversion of the card catalogue to computerized form in the nineteen-eighties and nineties. The project turned a profit, and proved a masterful plan to bring computers into the life of the library in the most persuasive way.

By the middle of the sixties, then, computers figured securely in the future of the library. In 1966, a ten-year forecast commissioned by Library Director Merle Fainsod and University Librarian Douglas Bryant projected a 1976 collection of more than ten million books, and a budget of $14.5 million or more. Amid calls for strengthening holdings in maps, archives, and other "non-book" materials and broadening collecting worldwide, the report also sounded a dire note:

> There are some who assert that computers and new techniques of electronic transmission of texts will shortly render existing libraries obsolete or at least enable them to reduce the extent of their holdings. As William S. Dix, the Princeton Librarian, recently wrote in his 1965 annual report, "It is easy to envision the world's store of books reduced to a quite small bulk by micro-reduction, controlled by a computer-stored catalogue which will give instant access to whatever is wanted by a scholar . . . transmitting to him instantly from the central store either an image of the printed text or a full-sized paper copy."

Fainsod and Bryant's report reasonably concludes that, over the coming decade, electronic texts will not become so inexpensive as to replace books, and that most of the library's expenditures will continue to relate to the purchase, care, and circulation of bound, paper-based objects. And yet, if the book would remain a secure medium, Widener's future—as an aging building in a time of diminishing budgets and the curricular marginalization of books—was not quite so certain.

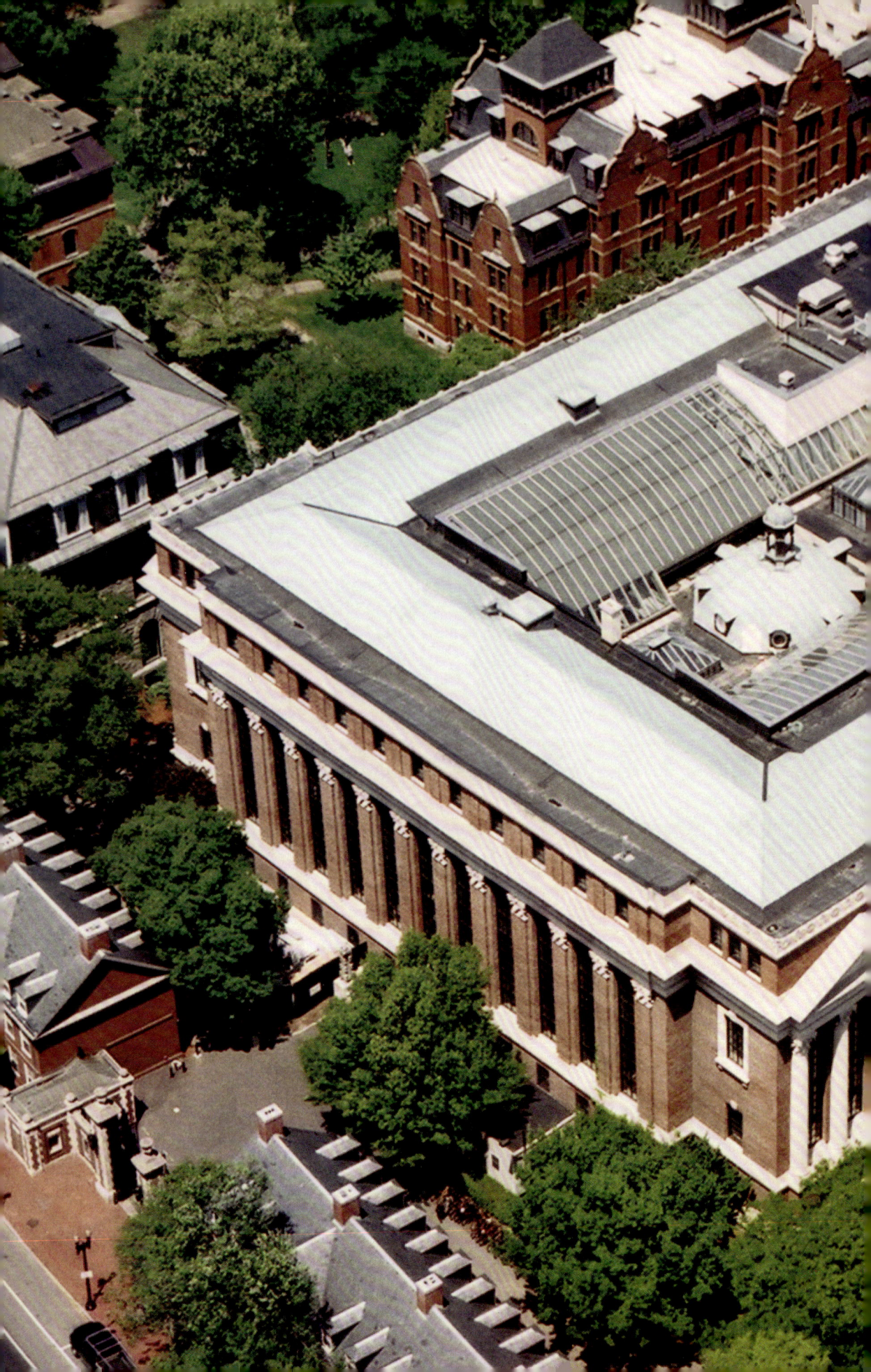

PART THREE
MONUMENTALLY INVITING

Widener looms over one of Gore Hall's two surviving Gothic finials, which flank the library's Massachusetts Avenue door.

On 23 May 1977, Harvard College Librarian Louis Martin received an envelope marked "to be opened only by the Director." It contained a handwritten note with dismaying news:

> Missing Widener books by the hundreds may be located in an office in the Vanserg Building. The utmost discretion and skill should be used in apprehending the occupant, and speed is also essential.
>
> Your checkout system, which has facilitated such massive and systematic theft, is incredibly poor.
>
> Please do not reveal that you were tipped off. The suspect is a pathological liar and would stop at no libel or slander to defend himself.

Martin immediately called for a meeting with Harvard University Police detectives, who decided to inspect Vanserg at 5 o'clock the following morning. Upon opening room 204, they found thousands of books, many stamped with a forged legend reading "Released–Harvard College Library." A review of the catalogue showed that the books had not been checked out or released from the collection. The rooms in Vanserg were occupied by Jeffrey Nelson, a graduate student in American History; esteemed in his department and well-liked by Widener staff, he was due to receive his Ph.D. just a few weeks later in June.

Altogether, investigators found almost five thousand books in Nelson's Vanserg hoard. Fourteen hundred of them came from Widener, with the balance coming from libraries in the U.S. and Britain. Nelson had evidently fabricated stamps reading

"Harvard College Library," "Harvard Law Library," "Released," and "Withdrawn." Nelson later said he had not planned to take the books from Harvard, but had become nervous about having to return such large numbers of books before leaving Cambridge upon his impending graduation. Nelson also referred to a host of medical problems, including psychiatric troubles, which he said had made trips to the library difficult. While faculty dithered over what sanction to impose, Nelson resigned an appointment he had received at Claremont College; he did not receive his doctorate.

In a way, the Nelson book-theft case provides an image of the exhaustion of Widener, Harvard, and the country in the wake of the tumult of the sixties. It was strikingly different from earlier Widener burglaries: Vito Aras's attempt on Widener's Gutenberg Bible in 1969, for instance, at the height of the sixties' campus chaos, was in its perverse way a grand and psychedelic gesture. A long and tiresome decade later, Nelson accumulated a horde of run-of-the-mill texts through a mixture of ennervation, exhaustion, and anxiety.

And so it was, even at the highest administrative levels. In 1976, President Derek Bok's *Annual Report* noted that library acquisitions had fallen five percent short of the number of volumes predicted a decade earlier. And the number of staff, though it had grown significantly, was off ten percent from levels projected in 1966. Due to inflation, costs had outstripped the library's budget. Available funds for book purchases were ten percent short of the predicted level, while personnel costs were seven percent higher than the library's administrators had expected back in 1966. Bok's report did not, however, note that the direst predictions of the 1966 report had not come to pass: the library still collected books by the ten thousands. The digital revolution remained on the horizon.

In the nineteen-eighties and nineties, however, Widener, like Harvard as a whole, underwent changes that were nothing short of revolutionary. To be sure, it was an era of rapid technological progress; but changes on the national and world stages impacted the University as well. The last two decades of the twentieth century would see the end of the communist era in Eastern Europe;

at home, the country underwent ideological and cultural shifts the likes of which had not been seen since the nineteen-thirties. Widener librarians strove throughout to collect the books, periodicals, bulletins, registers, statistical briefs, and ephemera that would document the era. As traditionalist academics battled with younger, theoretically-inclined colleagues both for control of humanities departments and a share of public discourse, as the rapid development of biotechnology ushered in new problems in science and in ethics, the aims of education emerged as a topic in the media. And those media, for their part, grew in complexity and power as well; in American society, the library saw its pre-eminence as a source of information threatened with eclipse.

For the university in the midst of such excitement, it was a time of unprecedented wealth. Extensive fundraising campaigns under presidents Derek Bok and Neil Rudenstine grew the university's endowment by geometric proportions. At the time of the Tercentenary in 1936, Harvard's endowment had contained $143 million; by the 350th anniversary in 1986, it had passed the billion dollar mark on its way to $20 billion by century's end. While the Corporation remained conservative, even miserly in its payouts to the University's many tubs, Harvard's considerable success in fundraising made possible a bewildering array of new programs in the library and beyond.

Widener's most portentous transformations, however, were technological. The digital version of the catalog card, known as a machine-readable catalog record, or MARC record, was little changed from the form it had taken nearly thirty years before. In it, title, author, publisher, date of publication, page count, and all the other bibiliographic data recorded on cards was "tagged" with cryptic code which, while arbitrary and impenetrable to the uninitiated, was simple for a computer to store and interpret. When Harvard joined the MARC pilot project in the sixties, there wasn't any simple way to use such records; the computers could only store and track the information; presenting it to library patrons in any form other than unreadable MARC-speak was not possible. By the mid-nineteen-seventies, Widener's cataloging department boasted two computer terminals with access to Fred Kilgour's OCLC–an Ohio-based service compiling a database of bibliographic records which, in twenty years' time, would become the largest single source of library data in the world (OCLC changed its formal name to Online Computer Library Center once its dominance in library record production reached around the world). But through the mid-nineteen-seventies, computerization progressed slowly–and not only in cataloging. A new digital system for recording loans had to be scrapped in the middle of development because the university abruptly adopted ID cards with magnetic stripes, a feature which the proposed library system could not accommodate.

OCLC, MARC–patrons then as now were largely unaware of the meaning of such library esoterica. As early as 1975, however, the spectre of the digital revolution loomed in Widener. With automation would come increasing demands for systematicity across libraries at Harvard and beyond; the growing databases of bibliographic information would need to speak to one another from library to library, and they needed to share a common language. But Widener's classification system, which had grown up through the late nineteenth century and matured under the watchful eye of Archibald Cary Coolidge, was a dialect unto its own, radically different from the Library of Congress system that was winning its long contest with Dewey to be accepted as the lingua franca of the library world.

The LC and Widener classification systems' differences weren't accidental; they reflected competing theories of knowledge. LC was disciplinary in structure, its classification defined by topic. Any given grouping contained books in numerous languages. The Widener system, however, emphasized language and country over discipline and topic, valuing the continuity of national knowledges. In many Widener classifications, works on a given country's history were followed by the national literature (although the major languages' literatures had classifications of their own, denominated by decimal numbers). The Widener system respected authors, too, striving to keep their works together, where LC would divide books by one author into several classes by subject matter. In a sense, the Widener system was Aristotelian; its divisions were empirical, describing and reflecting the languages and cultural origins of books and highlighting their relations to one another in language, place, and time; LC, by contrast, was Platonic, looking past the surface of language and nation to reflect the idealized, essential discipline in which each book, pamphlet, or periodical might be said to belong.

Still, with the online catalog on the horizon, Widener catalogers felt pressure to convert to LC. While the new computerized records, in MARC format, accommodated Widener call numbers as easily as they did LC, most records produced at other institutions would speak LC. Thus, Harvard would not be able to take advantage of electronic records available online. But the adoption of LC standards would only lower costs if the Library of Congress acquired and swiftly cataloged most of the books that Harvard bought. But in the mid-seventies, this wasn't the case in all areas. Searching the LC catalog, librarians in Widener Slavic Division discovered that the Library of Congress had failed to order fully ninety percent of the books they had acquired for Widener in 1976. Whether they switched to LC classes or not, Widener librarians would continue to do original cataloging for many—in some cases all—of the library's acquisitions.

Even if the LC system would work for patrons and catalogers, switching from the Widener system would not be simple. Converting all of Harvard's catalog records—about six million of them in 1975—was a daunting prospect. And by the mid-nineteen-seventies, Widener's cataloging backlog—the stock of books received by the library that remained uncataloged—had reached forty thousand volumes, larger than the library's yearly intake of about 32,000 volumes. A region of D-level was set aside for them—a shadow library within Widener residing in the basement; by the mid-nineteen-eighties, it would swell to nearly 150,000 volumes. Scholars could request these books—but would do so only if they already knew that the books they wanted were there, awaiting cataloging.

When Widener eventually adopted LC classifications, it did so only for newly acquired books. In the decades following the adoption of LC, interrelated books classed in the old and new

Monumentally Inviting

systems shadowed one another in the stacks, migrating to different sections and levels, leading scholars on often exhausting searches. Patrons now crossed levels and climbed stairs to find Widener-classed books and their LC counterparts.

Of course, not all the confusion could be ascribed to the Widener/LC dichotomy. While the bookstock grew, the academy changed; humanistic disciplines that once stood at the heart of the academic enterprise found their position contested as public policy studies and the social sciences rose to prominence. Jan Ziolkowski, Latinist and faculty member, wrote of disjunctions that manifest themselves in the late twentieth century: "What must have been a heavenly juxtaposition of Church documents on the sixth floor and Classical and Medieval Latin on the fifth floor has turned into a brutal estrangement: the woebegone library-user who wishes to integrate the Classical Latin world with its Christian Latin successor must be prepared for the aerobic experience of going up or down nine stories and negotiating perhaps a hundred yards between Widener and Pusey; and the person who wants to compare Midrash with Christian exegetic writings has an even longer trek to make."

But if the perambulations of Church historians increased in length in the nineteen-eighties and nineties, the speed and memory capacity of computers continued to grow at an even faster rate; and in the library world, systems at last emerged that could quickly search MARC data, crunch it into a form human beings could read, and spit it out from screen and printer. In libraries everywhere, terminals began to appear beside the cabinets of the card catalogues; patrons quickly learned to enter keywords and receive readable catalogue records in return.

Nineteen-eighty-five saw the birth of Harvard's online catalogue, HOLLIS. Although nominally an acronym—Harvard Online Library Information System—the name also recognized the contribution of Harvard's first library benefactors, the Hollis family, who throughout the eighteenth century sent books, money, and advice from London to the college at the edge of the wilderness (one of the funds they gave still buys books to this day). Of course, HOLLIS offered readers only the capacity to search MARC records, and at that time few books had them. To search books Harvard purchased before 1980, readers still consulted the card catalogs. Later, records produced from HOLLIS were printed as microfiche, sets of which were distributed to libraries at Harvard and made available for purchase by other institutions. This Distributable Union Catalog, or DUC, was the first attempt at making the powerful record-management tools of HOLLIS available to library patrons. And while it made it possible to search all of Harvard's current library records from off-site, it was an unwieldy and labor-intensive tool for the patron to use, and could not reflect the richness of Harvard's growing collections in real-time, as even the card catalog could do.

HOLLIS "went live" with some 410,000 records available from 132 terminals throughout the university library. Initially, only staff accessed the system, which primarily served as a tool for library workers engaged in the hectic business of buying, cataloging, tracking, and loaning books. Through its technical functions, staff coordinated the purchase, circulation, and physical status of books in the library in one system, allowing them to discover immediately if a needed book was owned or on order in any of Harvard's libraries—and if necessary order the book, debit the price from any acquisitions fund, and prompt the finance office to pay the vendor for the book. This coordination of the library's disparate information streams was one of the largely unappreciated triumphs of library automation. Most of those who lamented the loss of the card catalogues were unaware of these facets of library work and the triumph their automation represented. Students and scholars, for their part, still relied on the cards—or on the so-called Distributable Union Catalog, which displayed records printed from the HOLLIS database in flip-folders of microfilm cards, or fiche; the whole set resided in a flip-folder that sat near a fiche reader in every reference department in the university's libraries. While comprehensive, and remarkably effective—and expensive—as a means of safeguarding the catalogue, the flimsy fiche were maddening, fatiguing, and ill-suited to the free-form knowledge surfing that card catalogues had enabled long before the advent of the World Wide Web. And yet the DUC, for all its problems, was a terrific achievement, paving the way for the transformation of HOLLIS from an administrative tool to an engine of intellectual discovery.

Nearly five years in the making, HOLLIS was a project on a scale unprecedented in the library. In marked contrast to the initial forays into automation in the sixties and seventies, which for all their importance were trial balloons, the architecture of HOLLIS in its way was every bit as monumental as that of Widener (although Widener took less time to build).

The rest of the library world, meanwhile, had begun to turn their old card catalogs into databases of MARC records in a worldwide move to replace libraries' ubiquitous card cabinets with searchable computerized catalogs. A necessarily cautious Harvard belatedly followed suit, and in 1994 began to convert its card catalogue into MARC records. Throughout the mid-nineties, Harvard sent twenty thousand cards a week to OCLC, where they were checked against an enormous database of existing records and replaced with either the existing record or, about one-third of the time in Harvard's case, were given a brand-new record (which itself joined OCLC's sprawling database, soon the world's main repository of library records). Dubbed "Recon," the project would consign some five million catalogue cards, most from Widener, to obsolescence.

To make this burgeoning crop of digital bibliography available to users, Widener underwent yet another storm of changes. In 1989, wiring and cabling expanded throughout the building. Soon came the computers themselves, which would each year henceforward appear in new configurations, in new patterns and places. The iridescence of a screen suddenly would bloom among the dim lamps of the Reading Room; soon, whole tables were given over to them, where they sat glaring at each other across empty Windsor chairs. In the stacks, they would sprout here and there—behind an elevator, perhaps, or on a table near a window—each generation featuring a throbbing new graphic or dizzying screen-saver that would oscillate in the calm among the bookshelves. And suddenly they were ubiquitous—like vases of flowers, or typewriters, or carrousels of ink stamps, they took their place among the commonplace furniture of the library. What began as a few machines with flickering yellow displays grew to dozens and ultimately hundreds of terminals in Widener busily engaged in creating, modifying, correcting, and processing catalogue records—and ultimately serving them up to Widener's insatiably, restlessly curious readers.

Of course, they weren't proliferating in Widener alone. Soon, computers were in the offices and homes and dorm rooms of every searcher on campus and off—the library had cracked open; its secret spilled out into the ether, the precious, esoteric work of reading and pondering now spilled into the domestic multiverse. And as the word became at once more intimate and more intangible, the space in which its work had taken place—the library—seemed to diminish in both its practical and its ritual centrality.

AND AS EVER, THE LIBRARY REMAINED TOO SMALL. IN 1983, Library Director Oscar Handlin had proposed building the Harvard Depository. Opening just three years later, the depository quickly became known to faculty and staff as HD. It was designed to solve Harvard's library space problems once and for all; its six-acre site, in Southborough, Massachusetts, gives space enough to build as many as ten vast warehouses, each of which is capable of holding two million books. Today, the inner spaces of each of HD's storage units feels like a cavern of books—a rich and randomized vein opened deep in the earth. Its thirty-foot-high stack is tended by library workers riding mobile lifts that sail up and down the long aisles. As they arrive, the books are packed densely into trays that minimize the abrasion of books as they are shelved and reshelved. Patrons order them in Widener one day and receive them the next.

But the building of a vast new storage facility had left one question unanswered: which books would go there? President Eliot's "dead books" proposal, despite its objectionable flavor, had held sway when Keyes Metcalf opened NEDL in the nineteen-forties: the books that went to the old depository were old themselves, and little-used. Some had seen no use in decades; others had never been checked out at all. But with their storage offsite, their continued obsolesence was virtually assured. As HD opened in 1986, librarians and faculty members voiced concern that valuable nuggets of unmined scholarship might be buried forever in Southborough's glimmering caves of books. As acquisitions librarian Assunta Pisani observed in her department's 1985 annual report, the transfer of new and uncataloged books–the source of Widener's growing backlog–could effectively render such books inaccessible to scholarship. "From the point of view of national cooperation," she noted, the library would be "renouncing the unique contribution we could make to the nation's scholarly resources." Many of Pisani's colleagues, meanwhile, joined faculty in their concern that the potential of the stacks to foster serendipitous discoveries would be compromised by the storage of so many obscure books. And with the ever-present prospect of digitization looming on the horizon, some worried that HD would prove to be the first step in the effective eradication of books from the life of the academy.

In response, Kenneth E. Carpenter, an assistant director in the Harvard University Library, set up shop in Widener, where he began to work patiently with concerned faculty to develop criteria for selecting books that would preserve the scholarly record and the possibility of serendipity in the stacks. Carpenter entered librarianship as a stack page in Houghton Library; later, graduate study in Russian history and library school would prepare him for a career straddling the realms of scholarship and library work. By the time he began his work selecting books in Widener, he had catalogued Western books in Japan, curated the Kress Library at the Harvard Business School, compiled bibliographies of early economics texts, and published widely in library history. Faculty accepted him as a colleague with an intellectual sensibility broad enough to take in the nuances of their given fields. Carpenter's criteria reflected the peculiar demands of each of the many subjects areas addressed in Widener's collection. In one classification, he would take care to keep representative texts of all authors on the shelves; in another, bibliographies might suffice to record secondary or minor works. In certain fields, information was so time-sensitive that books even a decade old could safely be stored in HD. By fine-tuning his criteria to the demands of scholars, Carpenter was able to send seventy thousand books a year to HD without ruffling too many feathers.

By the nineteen-nineties, technology was making monthly leaps forward. HOLLIS was by now a viable online catalogue–though for books acquired before 1980, patrons were still consulting the card catalogue; some were driven to the painful trial of reading microfilmed records from the clumsy, pockmarked fiche of the DUC. In 1990, Richard De Gennaro had assumed the post of Librarian of Harvard College. De Gennaro had long experience with Widener and with technology; as associate librarian in the nineteen-sixties and seventies, he had been responsible for many of the library's early attempts at computer automation. In the mid-nineteen-sixties, in particular, he had moved agressively to incorporate technology into library work, using a computer to convert Widener's old shelflists into printable catalogs. The project turned a profit, and was one of the first to move computerization in the library beyond the experimental stage. His appointment signalled Harvard's commitment to the digital revolution in the library. In his 1992 *Annual Report*, meanwhile, President Neil Rudenstine sounded the apocalyptic note which by now had become familiar regarding the future of libraries: "It has essentially become impossible to talk about libraries, and to plan for their future, without also taking into account the present pace of technological change. . . . The library of the future will differ markedly from the libraries of the past. . . . a library will be–indeed, it is already being–conceived less as a single discrete physical space than as a gateway to a complex of networks . . . ."

And yet, while technology had entered the state of flux from which it has yet to emerge, in the nineteen-nineties it was Widener's physical state that was most symbolic of Rudenstine's gloomy forecast. Space for books and library work was indeed imperiled. In addition to the classificatory confusion of the stacks, the accretions of nearly a century's worth of renovations to the building–not to mention transformations in the worlds of library work and scholarship–had turned Widener's public areas into a maze of mysterious doors and rooms off-limits to readers.

The grand spaces for reading and study—the majestic main reading room, as well as reading rooms for government and economics, for rare books, for poetry and classics and recreational reading—had either disappeared altogether or been transformed into shrunken, fluorescent-lit ghosts of their former selves; more significantly, they no longer resonated with students who found searching for information from the privacy of their dorm rooms more comfortable. The work of Widener for nearly two decades had been the translation of physical objects bearing meaningful marks into transmittable bits. But the things those bits represented—the books—were imperiled. Increasingly derided as irrelevant to the information age, they sat in dusty stacks that were too hot, too dry, or too wet, too often exposed to light. Books had reached their reckoning moment—it was time either to dispense with them radically or to affirm their centrality for coming generations of scholars. Throughout academe, books were forced into competition with computers in a zero-sum game for budgetary prominence. Rather than see the complementarity of books and digital media, many chose to frame their relation in competitive terms; the end of the book, predicted at least as early as the nineteen-sixties, now seemed certain.

In 1996, the Harvard College Library commissioned an environmental study of Widener. The resulting report found numerous problems imperiling the collections: wide fluctuations in humidity and temperature, particulate and gaseous contamination that eroded paper and bindings, strong sunlight in some areas, and lack of control over the environment overall. In the old air handling system, there were no ducts; air drawn in from the outside entered the lowest levels and was drawn up through the toeholes at the base of each range of shelving to top of the stack, where exhaust fans removed it from the building. But in the late twentieth century, even this primitive ventilation system no longer worked. The fans were largely inoperable; heating was supplied by radiators and ventilation via the windows. From season to season, Widener's internal climate was more like the Mediterranean than New England: in summer, stifling humidity with temperatures in upper stack levels that reached into the nineties; in winter, sciroccos of dry, radiator-heated air in the daytime mixed with plummeting temperatures at night. Along with generous windows, the light courts—which had been incorporated in the original design primarily to provide daylight to the Memorial Rooms—admitted so much damaging light to the stacks that books at the ends of shelves were sunburned, tattooed and faded with the silhouette of the iron shelving armatures. And librarians realized that toeholes meant to keep the air circulating would circulate fire at least as effectively, threatening to turn a small blaze into a conflagration involving every level of the stack.

Widener's reckoning came the same year Nancy Cline was appointed Librarian of Harvard College. If Richard De Gennaro's mandate had been to force the library's transition into the digital era, Nancy's Cline's chief mission would be to integrate the new, digital dimensions of information into the life of the library. Along the way, the challenge would be to reaffirm Widener's—and all of the Harvard College Library's—role as the place where Harvard kept, conserved, and (no less importantly) celebrated the central place of books in the life of the university. The challenge was thus twofold: on one hand, to ameliorate the building's many problems in light, ventilation, security, and conservation; on the other hand, to return Widener to its original character as a hub for reading and research, to reclaim for readers space lost to the burgeoning technical services quartered in the library. In practice, of course, the difference between Cline's and De Gennaro's mandates was not so clear-cut; the building had seen small-scale renovations during De Gennaro's time, and any comprehensive renewal of Widener at the end of the twentieth century necessarily would have a large technological component. Ultimately, however, the renovation of Widener, as it rededicated the library to the occasion of reading, would transcend the dichotomy of Building and Bytes.

The rigors of the digital revolution, meanwhile, had left Widener staff feeling a mixture of elation and fatigue. The library world had risen to the challenge of the information age, engaging fundamental issues in the worlds of technology, society, and public policy. From the closing of card catalogs to questions about free access to information, libraries had received a great deal of public attention and criticism—far more, indeed, than they were accustomed to receiving. Some staff welcomed critical appraisal by commentators such as Nicholson Baker, whose long essays about online catalogs and the transformations of public libraries had found receptive audiences in the *New Yorker* magazine; the tensions and pressure of such attention, however, only added to the anxiety that such immense projects as the introduction of online catalogs and the conversion of the card catalog naturally produce. Many on the faculty, too, had been skeptical of HOLLIS and the advent of the Harvard Depository; and even librarians who defended the need for automation and the depository often shared these fears. In the midst of such a time, when the long-anticipated apocalypse of a paperless society seemed on the horizon, many feared that a renovation of Harvard's flagship library would result in a building that symbolized the diminishing importance of reading. Widener began its life as a memorial to a bibliophile—but would it end its days as a memorial to the book itself?

IN 1999, CLINE RECEIVED APPROVAL FROM PRESIDENT NEIL Rudenstine and Jeremy Knowles, Dean of the Faculty of Arts and Sciences, to begin a renovation of Widener that would address the threat to collections posed by the deteriorated state of the stack area. The Faculty of Arts and Sciences and the library together chose the architectural firm of Einhorn, Yaffee, Prescott, who had much experience renovating libraries and public buildings; the contractor was Lee Kennedy Company, a firm that had proven in the past its ability to pursue complex construction problems in facilities that remain open to the public. At first, the project was conceived strictly in terms of improvements in conditions for books; called the Widener Stack Renovation, design and engineering focused on the many problems of Widener's space for book storage. But it quickly became apparent that such improvements would cause sweeping changes throughout the public spaces of the building as well. New cabling and computer workstations would need to be installed; smoke detectors, sprinklers, and air ducts would need to interlace with the books; vast new machines would be needed to drive a system capable of supplying cool, dry air to the stacks year-round.

The logical place for these extensive systems was in the light courts. By roofing the courts over with skylights, furthermore, light could still penetrate to the memorial rooms while being filtered to remove the most damaging, ultraviolet end of the spectrum. But while building in the light courts might have seemed the most practical option, the prospect was potentially volatile. Perhaps the most famous provision of Eleanor's gift had been the decree that the building's exterior remain unaltered—and the light courts had always constituted an ambiguous middle ground between exterior and interior. These vacant spaces presented a mystery to Widener's staff—although frequently in view from windows in offices and the inner wall of the stack, they were off-limits. Except for Vito Aras's mad cat burglary, almost no one had ever visited them; their rough concrete floors, but for the rust-brown grilles of their drains, remained blank and untrodden.

Nancy Cline

Fortunately, this was not the first time the Widener family had been asked for permission to build in the light courts. Keyes Metcalf had considered the question upon his arrival at Harvard in 1937, but had abandoned the prospect largely due to sensitivity to Eleanor Widener's probable reaction to the proposal. The light courts came up again in the early nineteen-sixties, when a project to carry the two lowest levels of the stack into the light courts was proposed. This time, the Widener family responded favorably. In a letter addressed to the President and Fellows of Harvard College, the family's lawyers noted that provisions of the gift "evidence Mrs. Widener's interest and concern that the building should both house 'the general library of Harvard' and house her son's books. . . . Thinking of the rooms set aside for her son's books she stipulated that no changes, additions, or alterations be made, and 'particularly' that the courts which are on two sides of his rooms should be 'kept open for light and air.'" They added that "[a]n extension of a number of the lower floors in the manner suggested would add greatly to the utility of the building as a library and would not interfere in any degree with the light and air which the courts offer her son's room and the approaches to them," concluding that "the suggested extension of these floors will further Mrs. Widener's expressed wish and intention that the building should house 'the general library of Harvard' and will not conflict with her concern that her son's rooms be always as she planned them."

Harry's siblings, Eleanor Widener Dixon and George D. Widener, signed their attorneys' letter, stating that they were in accord with the plan to extend Widener's lower floors into the light courts. A that time, however, the plan was set aside—not because of objections from the family, but only because funds were too scarce. Revived in the nineteen-nineties, the plan to build reading rooms in the light courts would prove the most public and dynamic of the changes Widener underwent in its most thoroughgoing renovation.

WIDENER HAD SURVIVED THE TRANSFORMATIONS OF THE twentieth century by transforming itself. As the Harvard College Library expanded throughout the Yard, as its collection proliferated, Widener went from being "the" University Library to the command center of a vast array of systems, staffs, and resources. Vacated studies became staff offices, and reading rooms, such as the Government and Economics Reading Room on the ground floor and the Treasure Room on level one, sprouted cubicles as

Widener's staff of catalogers and book-processors of all kinds grew. When the card catalog cabinets moved into the corridors of the third floor, their real estate was occupied by book acquisitors and the technicians who sent books to HD. In the stacks, numerous carrels were adopted by a busy staff striving to keep up with the demands of Widener's ever-burgeoning book stock.

But if Widener's importance drove the demand for a thorough renovation, it also presented a problem, for the building could not realistically be closed for any length of time. Its collections were too important to scholarship in nearly every faculty and division; furthermore, they were too large to house elsewhere. Archibald Cary Coolidge's once-laughable proposal to house books in the Stadium might now have seemed plausible; only the Stadium was large enough. More practical possibilities were considered, only to be rejected: sending the collection to HD in stages was unpalatable to librarians and faculty alike.

Eventually, a plan emerged: called the HD Push Project and placed under the direction of Marilyn Wood, the Widener librarian who administered the transmission of Ken Carpenter's selections to HD, it would send a vast number of books to the Depository, creating a moveable "swing space" in the stacks. Ken Carpenter's efforts already were sending out seventy thousand books annually; now, in the two years before active construction began, a specially-hired team would send half a million books to HD—nearly as many books as the new Widener held on its opening day. To do so, the team worked in two daily shifts pulling books from the stacks, relying on the criteria—and the faculty goodwill—that Ken Carpenter had developed over the previous years, as well as a host of sophisticated reports from HOLLIS. By the time the renovation was underway, the HD Push Project had carefully selected five hundred thousand books, modified (and in many cases improved) their catalog records, and sent to them to Southborough, where, along with three million other books—a Widener's worth—they are available to Widener patrons with twenty-four hours' notice.

With space in the stacks now open and flexible, Heads of Stack Ron Tesler and Johnny Weyand devised a plan for moving and

During the "HD Push" project, Widener staff settled into temporary work stations in the former Catalog Room, where they sent 500,000 books to the Depository in two years' time.

reshelving books to make way for construction, one half-level at a time. As each half-level was completed, the books migrated into successively emptied stack levels in an enormous, three-dimensional chess game. Every three weeks, book shelvers under the supervision of the library's Operations Director Paul Bellenoit moved 150,000 books—monthly undertakings on the order of magnitude of Frank Carney's great shifting of the books out of Gore Hall nearly a century before.

FOR WIDENER STAFF, the renovation began slowly and—if I may say so—painfully. I began working in Widener in 1998; with the advent of the renovation looming, pre-construction projects were already cropping up in the recesses of the library. I worked on D-level—at the time, a booming, open space, still very much a cellar—where a colleague and I shared a long, narrow office on the central hallway that ran, through an opening framed in chicken wire, to the stacks. Workers of all kinds—carpenters, electricians, tin-knockers—

already were appearing with increasing frequency in the library's quiet halls. One day while returning to my office after going for coffee, I noticed that the door to D-level was ajar. Strange, I thought—it was typically locked, this door, as it gave on the Mass Ave. corridor near the entrance to the building. As I pulled the door fully open, I was dealt a shocking (albeit thankfully undamaging) blow to the head as a thick, dingy screwdriver rattled down the stairs before me. Rubbing my scalp, I plucked up the screwdriver by the shaft as if catching some sort of objectionable little rodent by the tail. Looking up, I realized that it had been stuck into the jamb to hold open the door.

Soon, other changes were apparent. My office looked onto the East light court through a window near the ceiling; though little sunshine reached this deep into the cavernous space, it provided a brightening glow even on wintry days when the court would swirl with snow. Then one day, a shed appeared in the far corner; soon, it filled up with long fascicles of steel bound like kindling. Not long thereafter, the windows were boarded up, and my colleague and I could only guess, from the sound of sawing and drilling, as well as from the hoarse shouts of the tradesmen, that big changes were afoot.

More changes followed. One morning, I arrived to find that my desk had been pushed a full ten feet closer to my colleague's workstation at the opposite end of the room; a new wall now stood in its old place, and everything in the room was covered in a fine layer of plaster dust. A couple of weeks later, the same phenomenon took place at the opposite end of the office; and then we were moving out, headed for new quarters upstairs while D-level received the renovation's full attention.

Scholars, too, were affected by the renovation. Throughout the project, books seemed to mill about like restless cattle in an immense pastureland; there was no telling, from week to week, where one's particular herd might be found grazing. The lines of tape in several colors, leading patrons from the stack entrance to Pusey and Lamont, were of little help; but library staff who worked in the stack soon devised ingenious signs to notify readers of changes and to help them find their way in what was, even in the most settled of times, a confusing labyrinth of books. One reader, looking for Widener's Fr (French history) class, found in their usual precinct on D-level only a sign notifying him that the books had moved, with an arrow pointing the direction in which they had travelled. Walking in the indicated direction to the other end of the level, he found another, simpler sign, inscribed "Fr" with an arrow pointing down a dark half range of books. Squeezing past the shelves, he found himself in a corner-cul-de-sac of shelves, standing before another sign. "The books are behind you," it read.

Such carefully-considered signage was a small part of a vast communication program that kept staff and library patrons apprised of the projects many phases. While the light courts were undergoing construction, closed-circuit television monitors in the Widener lunch room offered a window on the complex construction undertaken out of sight, but not out of earshot, of most staff. The monitors, along with kiosks near entryways, e-mail notices, and in-depth monthly briefings, took much of the mystery out of the cacaphony of drilling, pounding, and smashing that indicated that Widener, for now, was not only a research library, but also a building site, with as many as one hundred construction workers in the building at any one time.

While the lives of peregrinatory students and scholars were altered by the renovation, it was the library staff who bore the brunt of the project. Ultimately, winning the support of Widener's large, diverse, and accomplished staff, whose daily lives would be profoundly affected by construction as well as the shuffling of workspaces and books, would in the end prove a greater challenge than selling the renovation to faculty and students. An especially difficult blow came in December 2000, when a large contingent of highly trained catalogers and acquisitions staff with hard-won knowledge of Widener's collections were relocated to a new technical services facility in Central Square. Faculty approval of the renovation had been won with the pledge to return studies and reading space lost to the growth of staff and services in Widener over the course of the twentieth century. Although the transfer of so many staff out of Widener would make it possible to open new reading rooms and offer new services, it was a painful time for many staff whose working lives were so entwined with the building and Harvard Yard.

For those who remained, the challenges were as great. Not only had every book in Widener been moved; not only had every staff member changed offices and endured the migraine-spawning sound of drills, saws, and other heavy equipment; but along the way they learned to share the world's largest academic library with the tradespeople who worked from basement to rooftop to make Widener's transformation complete. To the steelworkers, carpenters, pipefitters, and construction engineers, the challenges were no less profound. Turning a working library into a construction site means setting up barriers, building temporary walls, and above all working carefully around the books. It also means enduring the constant scrutiny and skepticism of outsiders. For months, they laid pipe and knocked together tall, gleaming trees of ductwork under the curious eyes of Widener's scholars, students, and staff, who learned to appreciate their workmanship. So much expert work—these ducts tucked into cabinetwork and over the ranges of the stack, these plaited, arm-thick skeins of cable, these turned and polished conduits, these expertly aligned cork floors—so much art and craft has disappeared under plaster, under brick, or underfoot. This careful craftsmanship, like that of the original, anonymous workers who built Widener with steam shovels and wooden cranes, will be all but forgotten by the generations of scholars to come. It is to be hoped that this generation of staff will remember—and that their experience of Widener as a workplace will extend beyond a reverence for the collections to a lingering appreciation of artful arrangement of bricks, steel, wood, and circuitry that makes Widener a structure destined to endure.

The first substantial renovation work began in the light courts, where the floors would be demolished and excavated and concrete poured to serve as a fresh base for the new machine rooms and the airy, light-filled reading rooms that rise above the systems. For most readers, students, and casual observers, the project's beginning was heralded with the appearance of a looming

yellow crane that rose on its own foundation on the Massachusetts Avenue side of Widener. Trucked from Texas, the crane climbed into the sky over the course of a Spring afternoon in 1999; it took two smaller cranes to erect it. Soon, its long boom, like the second hand of a vast clock, was sweeping back and forth over the rooftops of Widener, its flying shadow now and again darkening the aisles of the stacks for readers and staff who stopped to gaze in wonder as it ferried steel, concrete, and caterpillar-tracked backhoes into the library's heart. Days soon came when the whole building shook with the sound of shovels and jackhammers, when hardhats seemed to outnumber the stocking caps of students and the porkpies of superannuated scholars alike.

Above: *One of Widener's light courts under reconstruction, with new ducts snaking their way up the wall of the Memorial Rooms.* Opposite: *The crane erected beside Widener by the Lee Kennedy construction company became a fixture of the library and Harvard Yard.*

For administrators, librarians, and construction workers, the renovation was more than simply a vast construction project: it was also a long-running seminar in the history of the building. One of the most evocative lessons came when workers uncovered a bronze plaque in a niche in the wall on level 2 in the stacks that read, "Here worked Addie Francis Rowe, (1860-1938), Friend and Aider of Scholars." A HOLLIS search revealed a small book in Widener, printed by the Harvard University Press in 1939, called *Addie Francis Rowe, a Biographical Sketch*. It told the story of a woman who had quietly flourished in study carrel 209 during Widener's first three decades. An editorial secretary, Miss Rowe had earned the respect and devotion of Hyder Rollins, Edward Channing, and other Harvard scholars whose books she patiently edited, corrected, and saw into print. Several of these eminent figures were so impressed by Miss Rowe's editorial talent and eccentric ways that they asked her to write a brief account of herself.

Like Frank Carney, Addie Francis Rowe was denied station and authority in turn-of-the century Harvard; class and education saw to that. And yet like Carney, Rowe tranformed herself into a scholar, carving out a quiet spot where she could pursue her own attenuated passions among Widener's books. Over the course of her career, Miss Rowe grew in a spectacular forest of geraniums in the sunny windows that lined her carrel in the East stack. In her own time, the towering plants were objects of fancy and speculation on the part of graduate students and staff who passed by and wondered about the small, strangely attired woman who labored obscurely amid the greenery. But the flowers faded after her lonely passing; the plaque and book commissioned by the scholars who relied on her labors had all but disappeared, too, until construction workers broke through a wall in the spring of 2001.

Other discoveries, while less moving, were no less instructive. When Nancy Cline's office ceiling was partially removed for wiring work, she discovered that fluorescent lighting installations had obscured ornate moldings. Operations Director Paul Bellenoit found himself similarly nonplussed at Widener's wonders. Bellenoit, who had come to the library from the Harvard Business School and would in time assume the mantle of Frank Carney and John Shea, was a seasoned expert in the construction field; the building still held surprises for him and the tradesmen whose work he oversaw. He now recalls with chagrin watching five-foot-long drill bits disappear into walls of solid brick, far thicker and more solidly built than modern practice would deem necessary. Cline and Bellenoit, along with the architects and contractors, quickly realized what a wealth of design features and construction elements had disappeared or been forgotten over the years. Skylights in the ceiling of the main Reading Room, once subtle panes of stained glass, were now concealed by ranks of fluorescent tubes; the catalogue room's parti-colored vaulted ceiling had been painted white, and had sprouted vast, hanging blocks of light fixtures; the ceilings of the main entrance hall were similarly obscured with tidy white paint and bland lighting. Although the book collection had long ago outgrown the stack, in truth it was the accoutrements of administration that had supplanted the monumental and celebratory in Widener's interior spaces. Although it began as an urgent project to safeguard the collections, Widener's twenty-first century renovation grew into a rethinking of the way staff and scholars used the spaces of the library and how those spaces affected them.

IN THE COURSE OF WIDENER'S RENOVATION, BUILDERS AND technicians have spent the last five years relocating about nine miles of electronic cable and installing three miles of fire alarm wires; they have removed 1,200 cubic yards of soil from light courts (with each cubic yard equal to about 208 gallons), and 105 tons of old ductwork; they have replaced four thousand light fixtures and one thousand switches in stacks; they have taken down and scrubbed clean some eight thousand shelves and have moved, cleaned, and reshelved 3.5 million books. And these figures, while they indicate the scope of the project, do little to illustrate the thousands of alterations and repairs they have invested on every floor of the buildng, in nearly every conceivable corner.

Such changes have altered life throughout Widener. In the stacks, the transformation is both subtle and profound. Ductwork needed to handle the rapid transfer of air is incorporated all-but invisibly into new study carrels, minimizing the amount of shelving that would be lost while providing study space for carrel-holders that is better lighted, wired, and more secure that the admittedly picturesque desks of old. Overhead, discrete fluorescent fix-

A peek into Reference Room (formerly the Catalog Room) gives a view of reference librarians and curious patrons.

tures replace the bare incandescents of old; when a reader enters the shelving range, they switch on automatically in the manner to which patrons of large open-stack libraries everywhere are now accustomed. The elevators, too, have changed; gone are the rides in the cramped old cars that rattled and swayed, thrilling the stack boys in Frank Carney's day and terrifying patrons in our own. But perhaps the most important change is the most subtle one. Everywhere one goes in the Widener stack, from D-level to the heights of level 6, the air is the same: cool, dry, sweet. Before the renovation, the upper floors smelled, in summer, of gently roasted books, while D-level year-round offered the sporiferous scent usually associated with grottoes and Roman cellars. It is easy to be nostalgic for the redolent atmosphere of the old stacks; but the books are better protected, bathed now in clean air.

Widener's basement, known as D level, is a world of its own, without natural light, with big spaces and heavy square columns. Imaging services, microfilming, and the Conservation Lab reside down here, in customized spaces where the staff can control the light precisely to suit their specialized needs. The likes of these highly trained craftspeople did not work in Widener when it opened; it's fitting that they now undo the damage of the building's past in what are perhaps its most carefully designed spaces.

The ground floor now concentrates the library basic services and labors: shipping and receiving, building management, and

The restored ceiling of Widener's Reference Room (above) brings back a splendor that had disappeared behind white paint and fluorescent light fixtures (below).

the operations that transfer books in and out of the library. The original Lower Reading Room on the ground floor, which had served as the space where books were stamped and labelled for shelving in the late twentieth century, now contains the offices of the human resources department.

An octagonal space beneath the Memorial Room that once housed the Archives now contains a state-of-the-art microtexts facility, with new microfilm machines that make reading and printing from microfilm almost painless and permit users to print, download, or e-mail images of pages they find useful. The old Treasure Room on the West side of the first floor, which for decades served as office space for catalogers, is a reading room once more; now home to Current Periodicals, it offers open, accessible shelving and comfortable seating. More dramatic changes, of course, have come in the light courts, where soaring, vaulted skylights overspread the library's two new and popular reading rooms. On the West side, the Stack Reading Room offers study space that is readily acces-

Above: *The Phillips Reading Room, one of two new reading rooms in the Widener light courts.*
Opposite page: *The restored main reading room, now named the Loker Reading Room.*

Monumentally Inviting   183

sible from the stack; to the East, the soaring space of the Phillips Room furnishes readers with ample room to consult rare and fragile items restricted to use in the building.

Climbing the main stairs, past Sargent's murals and the entrance to Harry's rooms, is today an ascent into a quieter realm. In the magnificent main reading room—now named the Loker Reading Room in honor of Katherine B. Loker, who gave generously to the renovation project—the skylights have been replaced, the ceiling restored to its original glory. Although Metcalf's proposed mezzanine never was built (despite its momentary revival by enterprising faculty in the nineties) the room had lost space in the areas beyond each colonnade at the ends of the room to shelving, staff desks, and storage; those two zones are now once again knit into the vast reading room. Now, readers choose from a forest of different spots for reading and reflection, from mid-room spots with wide vistas to corner glades and copses. The adjacent catalogue room has been turned into a reference area, removing the bustle of question and consultation from study areas. The room's panelling glows, and the ornate ceiling has been restored to its original, prismatic paint scheme.

The Memorial Rooms are undergoing restoration at this writing; their unveiling will mark the end of Widener's renovation. Superficially, little will have changed: the new drapes are a careful match to the old; heating, cooling, and ventilation are updated, and subtle security measures installed. With the skylights in the new reading rooms filtering the natural light that once fell in the light courts, Harry Elkins Widener's books are better protected from its ravages.

Work on the Memorial Rooms continues at this writing; by the time you read these words they will be open once again, as monumentally inviting as ever. For a short while longer, however, the door is shuttered with plywood—a promise of things to come, and a reminder that Widener is still full of doors waiting to be opened.

Postscript

"In the last decades of the nineteenth century," writes Harvard historian Oscar Handlin, "fresh impulses transformed the writing of American history. Until then history had been the avocation of gentlemanly scholars, journalists, and *litterateurs*, working as individuals. . . . Now it became a profession and found a recognized place, of growing consequence, as one of the rigorous disciplines in college curricula." By no means restricted to the writing of history, these fresh impulses were part of a pattern of inspiration that emerged throughout the American academy in the twentieth century. As Thorstein Veblen predicted, this rise in professionalism and prestige was both fruitful and fitful, energetic and problematic. And as we have seen, Widener was—as it continues to be—one of the chief scenes of this broadening of American intellectual aspiration.

In *The Uprooted*, the arresting book for which he won the Pulitzer Prize in 1951, Oscar Handlin told the story of those who emigrated from Europe to America. Like Widener's Frank Carney, Handlin is the son of such immigrants. Carney referred to a thatched-roof cottage in Country Tyrone, while Handlin writes of the "gray Ukrainian town" from which his own father departed for America. Along the line that connects these disparate places to one another and to the New World, Carney and Handlin's parents with countless others crossed a meridian—a line where night fell on the communal ways of Europe's uprooted peasants, who now faced the individualism and alienation of life in America. Handlin recounted the story of such immigrants and their children, who coped with this nightfall as they found fresh fields to till, new kinds of crops to sow. Carney and Handlin, of course, although they ended up in the same building, followed vastly different paths; and yet for both it must be said that Widener was a field that yielded most abundant harvests.

Oscar Handlin has practiced his craft at Harvard since joining the history department in 1939 (he received his Ph.D. from the university the following year). As a faculty member who depended on Widener, he experienced the changes of the Metcalf era and the transformations of the decades that followed. In the course of his career, the Harvard College Library outgrew Widener to become an archipelago of specialized repositories: Houghton, Lamont, and NEDL paved the way; joined with the Fogg Museum collection, Widener's art books left to form the Fine Arts Library, which became part of the Harvard College Library in 1962; Hilles, Radcliffe's library, was added in 1966; thereafter followed the Pusey Library, connecting Widener, Lamont, and Houghton underground; Cabot Science Library in 1973, Littauer and the Harvard Yenching Library in 1976; the Loeb Music Library in 1978, among others. At each stage, collections were uprooted–and yet Widener persevered, wonderfully undiminished.

But Oscar Handlin has known Widener not only as a scholar, patron, and habitué, but as its chief: from 1979 to 1985, as Carl M. Loeb University Professor, he served as Director of the University Library. He guided Harvard's library system during one of the most contentious periods described in this book. He witnessed–and helped to determine–the course of the library through its liberalization and diversification (in 1980 he oversaw the appointment of the first woman, Y. T. Feng, to the post of Harvard College Librarian); through the culture wars of the 1980s; through the emergence of new technologies that threatened to undermine not only the place of Widener at Harvard, but the role of the research library–and for that matter, of the book itself–in academic life.

Perhaps the single most important change Handlin directed, however, was the introduction of the Harvard Depository. Despite enormous resistance from colleagues throughout the university, Handlin implemented his vision. What seemed to some to presage the end of the library as we know it appears, in retrospect, to have saved it. Without the Harvard Depository, Widener would not have room sufficient for all its collections, growing now at nearly one hundred thousand volumes a year; it would not have continued as a center of dynamic research and an architectural celebration of reading and the *vita contemplativa*. It would have been replaced, and its replacement likely would have been reduced in scope and vision—less vexing perhaps than the original, but surely less inspiring as well.

In the essay quoted from earlier, Handlin observed that for the historian in the early twentieth century, fact trumped truth—the "larger truth" that had led earlier generations of historians to pass over in silence the uncomfortable, the exceptional, and the problematic. With the "obligation of scrupulous factual accuracy," however, came all the burdens of a modern profession: specialization, the systematization of training and accreditation, the proliferation of theory and sophisticated vocabularies. We see that this too has taken place in the life of the library. The challenge, now as at each other stage, has been to reaffirm the humanism, and possibly the humanity, of the library in the midst of rude shocks to its very identity.

Daily, Oscar Handlin still makes his way to his top-floor study in Widener Library—the apex of the study-holders' order, whither next only heaven, according to Widener lore—where he continues to read and write alongside his wife and co-author, Lilian. With his solid presence, his steady smile, and his equipage of cane and broad-brimmed hat, he makes his way down the elevators and out the Mass. Ave. door, emerging to blink in the sunlight, cutting a figure at once fleeting and familiar. It is this figure with which I wish to leave you—that of a scholar making his way into the light from amid the books he has helped to curate and conserve, and among which, bent and searching, he seeks out both the scrupulous facts and the larger truth.

Notes on Sources

The following notes omit citations whenever they are made explicit in the text. Rather than employ superscript numbers in the text, I have chosen to refer notes to the concluding three or four words of the citation. I use a number of abbreviations below, each of which is introduced parenthetically at the first instance of its use. I gratefully acknowledge the courtesy of the Harvard University Archives in granting permission to publish quotations from resources in their collection.

Page 1: "mass and weight of academic empire"; Bainbridge Bunting, *Harvard, an Architectural History*. Completed and edited by Margaret Henderson Floyd (Cambridge, MA: Belknap Press of the Harvard University Press 1985).

Page 2: "transparent institution"; Alistair Black, *A New History of the English Public Library, Social and Intellectual Contexts, 1850-1914* (London: Leicester University Press 1996).

Page 3-4: Chest of 1900, Frank Carney (FC) folder. Harvard University Archives (HUA), HUA 900.11.

Page 5: "walkways of the earlier campus": Bunting 43.

Page 5: "as early as 1863"; William Bentinck-Smith, *". . .a memorial to my dear son": Some Reflections on 65 Years of the Harry Elkins Widener Memorial Library* (Cambridge, MA: Harvard College Library 1980), pages 4-5.

Page 5: "abstained from expressing it"; Henry James, *The Bostonians*. New York: Penguin, 1984, page 244. I am grateful to Roger E. Stoddard for pointing out James's mention of Gore Hall.

Page 6: "filled to repletion"; Annual Report of the President of Harvard College (AR), 1877, page 105.

Page 6: "classed among the impossibilities"; FC, History of Shelving Department, HUA III 50.29.00.6.

Page 10: "those who are most interested in the College Library: Lane, Annual Report of the President (AR) 1903-04, page 209.

Page 11: "additional book storage": William Coolidge Lane (WCL) correspondence, HUA III 50.8.10.2, box 26.

Page 11-13: Charles William Eliot (CWE) to WCL, 21 June 1904. HUA III 50.8.10.2, box 26.

Page 13: *Scientific American*, 27 May 1911.

Pages 14-16: see Leslie Morris, "Harry Elkins Widener and A.S.W. Rosenbach: Of Books and Friendship." *Harvard Library Bulletin* (*HLB*) n.s. Volume 6 Number 4, Winter 1995, pages 7-28; Steven Biel, *Down With the Old Canoe: a Cultural History of the Titanic Disaster* (New York: W.W. Norton 1996).

Page 18: "dealer in New Jersey"; *Harvard Graduates' Magazine* volume 7 number 27, March 1899, pages 432-3.

Page 19: "as far as I know"; Archibald Cary Coolidge (ACC) Correspondence. HUA III 50.8.11.1, Walter Lichtenstein folder.

Page 20: "consultation of books"; Ephraim Emerton, "A Blot in the 'Scutcheon." *Harvard Graduates' Magazine* volume 7 number 28, June 1899.

Pages 20-21: "matter of fact"; Thorstein Veblen, *The Higher Learning in America* (New Brunswick, USA: Transaction 1993), page 9.

Page 22: "Cambridge, Mass, USA"; ACC biographical files, HUG 1299.7.

Page 23: "to feel virtuous"; A. Lawrence Lowell (ALL) to Rev'd William Lowell, March 1912. ALL correspondence, HUA I.5.160 2A.

Page 25: (lifeboat four); Philip Gowan, "Mrs. George Dunton Widener." *Encyclopedia Titanica* online (www.encyclopedia-titanica.org).

Page 27: "so often stated"; ALL correspondence, HUA I.5.160 2A.

Page 28: Abele; Dreck Spurlock Wilson, editor, *African-American Architects: A Biographical Dictionary, 1865-1945* (New York: Routledge 2004).

Pages 28-29: "narrowest possible limits"; Emerton to ACC 9/7/12. ACC correspondence, HUA III 50.8.11.1 box 6.

Pages 29-30: "these various divisions"; Benjamin Rand to President and Fellows, 5/24/12. ACC correspondence, HUA III 50.8.11.1, box 6.

Pages 30-31: "under the stadium"; ACC probably refers to historian Edward Channing (1856-1931). ACC correspondence, HUA III 50.8.11.1, box 6. "relation to one another"; FC, Building Superintendent Reports, Harvard University Archives, HUA III 50.15.22.5.

Pages 31-34: FC diary; HUA III. 50,29.12.3.

Page 35: "books of the 'Inferno'"; *Library Journal* (*LJ*), February 1913, page 84.

Page 36: "even above it"; WCL, Misc. papers and plans, 1923, HUA III 50.29.15.2.

Pages 37-38: "not abundant now"; ACC correspondence, HUA III 50.8.11.1, box 6.

Pages 38-39: "closely as we shall"; WCL, Misc. papers and plans, 1923, HUA III 50.29.15.2.

Page 40: "convenient as possible"; WCL to ACC 1/31/13[?], ACC correspondence, HUA III 50.8.11.3, box 6.

Pages 41-43: Deed of Trust; "a part thereof"; ALL correspondence, HUA I.5.160 2A.

Pages 42-45: "accordance with its surroundings . . . appearance to herself"; ibid.

Page 45: "verb. sap."; ibid. :committee of advisors"; ACC correspondence, HUA III 50.8.11.1 box 6.

Pages 45-46: "to me less important"; copy to ACC, ibid.

Page 46: into [the new library] every day"; Bentinck-Smith, *Building a Great Library*, page 82.

Page 46: "resewed by our binder"; Widener building superintendent reports, 1913-14. HUA III 50.15.22.5.

Page 47: "spring up armed men"; Address of Henry Cabot Lodge delivered at the Dedication of the Harry Elkins Widener Memorial Library, 24 June 1915. Typescript. Houghton Library, HEW 7.2.2.

Page 53: "young Harry Widener"; *LJ* May 1915.

Page 55: "not in use"; Widener Library building rules, HUA III 50.15.22.10.

Page 55: "the individual radiators"; FC's Widener notes, ibid.

Page 56: "Part of the stack"; ibid.

Pages 56-58: "consultation of books"; ibid.

Pages 58-59: "detriment of the elevators"; ibid.

Page 59: "thief was after"; ibid.

Pages 59-60: "provide more toilets"; ibid.

Page 60: "President Lowell's reports. . . . early in 1915"; Samuel Eliot Morison, *Three Centuries of Harvard* (Cambridge, MA: Belknap 1936), pages 450-1.

Page 61: "reaction and partisanship"; Veblen, *Higher Learning*.

Page 61: "service of students"; *LJ* 1915.

Page 67: "*pro patria mori*"; Wilfred Owen, *The Complete Poems and Fragments*, ed. by Jon Stallworthy (London: Chatto & Windus / Hogarth / Oxford 1983).

Page 67: "Henry Farnsworth loved"; Martin Gilbert, *The First World War: A Complete History* (New York: Henry Holt 1994), page 197.

Page 67: Farnsworth's experience in the trenches; see Edwin W. Morse, *The Vanguard of American Volunteers* (New York: Scribners 1919)

Page 69: "into their own"; Farnsworth Room scrap book, HUA III 50.15.141, ca. 6 December 1917. "voice of the room"; ibid.

Pages 69-70: "genius of the room"; ibid.

Page 70: "our handsome books'"; ibid.

Pages 70-72: "unlost or unheard"; Henry James, "The Great Good Place," ibid; the story is included in many anthologies, including Henry James, *Complete Stories, 1898-1910* (New York: Library of America 1996).

Page 72: "echoes it somewhat"; ibid., March 16, 1917.

Page 72: "professors and students"; *LJ* May 1915.

Pages 72-74: "same one as before"; ACC Correspondence, HUA III 50.8.11.1, box 6; folder: "Studies: Individual Requests 1912-1918"; "and are irreplaceable"; ibid.; "Mercier in with you"; ibid; "conspicuously little success"; ibid.

Page 75: requests for space in Widener stacks by department; "wish to work there"; ibid.

Pages 76-78: "volumes were shipped"; detriment of the elevator"; "to women cleaners"; FC Building Superintendent Reports, 1918, HUA III 50.15 22.5.

Pages 78-86: WCL, general correspondence file, 1897-1928, HUA III 50.8.10.2, box 26, folders "library discipline A-M" and "N-Z."

Pages 88-89: newspaper clippings in theft case file, 1931-31, HUA III 50.29.31

Page 92: building in Lowell's time; see John Bethell, *Harvard Observed* (Cambridge, MA: Harvard 1998), pages 112-113.

Pages 95-96: Keyes Dewitt Metcalf (KDM) at Oberlin, see www.oberlin.edu/archive/holdings/finding /RG30/SG212/adminhist.htm.

Pages 96-97: KDM appointment; see Edwin E. Williams, "The Metcalf Administration," *HLB* 17 (1969), pages 113-130.

Pages 98-100: *Harvard Crimson* (*HC*) articles: "contributions to their fields," "all human warmth"; 16 October 1937. "tells it with a smile"; 14 October 1937. "future of Harvard College," "basements of Widener"; 18 November 1937. Library wage issues, see *Harvard Monthly* 23 November 1937.

Page 102: "Widener is becoming critical"; "program of the Library"; KDM in AR 1937-8, page 341. "specific nutrient materials"; "heritage of our civilization"; JBC, ibid., pages 5, 7.

Pages 103-104: "undoubtedly been made available"; KDM, *My Harvard Library Years, 1937-1955* (Cambridge, MA: Harvard College Library 1988), page 27.

Page 104: "overnight use only"; KDM Papers, HUA III 50.8.11.3, box 47, "reserves" folder.

Page 105: D.W. Prall, Douglas Bush, Kenneth B. Murdock, André Moorize, Derwent Whittlesley; ibid.

Page 106: "library is improved"; ibid.

Page 106: "handled until 1969"; James Bryant Conant (JBC) papers, HUA I 5.168, "Widener Library, 1938-39" file.

Page 107: "eight to ten years"; ibid.

Page 109: "so far as I know"; KDM papers, HUA III 50.8.11.3, box 21, "T. Frank Currier" folder.

Page 110: "others travel therein"; "capitalize German nouns"; ibid.

Pages 110-111: "[signed] Laura Hibbard"; KDM papers, HUA III 50.8.11.3, box 47, "Houghton and Treasure Room" folder.

Pages 111-112: "remarks of their friends"; KDM papers, HUA III 50.8.11.3, box 47, S folder.

Pages 112-113: "Henrietta M. Larson"; KDM papers, HUA III 50.8.11.3, box 46.

Page 114: "opened to Radcliffe students"; ibid.

Page 114: "staff follow suit"; ibid.

Page 115: "half of 1958 on"; Paul Buck, "A New Personnel Program for Harvard Librarians," *HLB* 12:3 (1958), page 296. "in the lunchroom," "serve as hostess"; papers relating to afternoon tea, 1944-46, HUA III 50.29.44.5.

Page 116: "next three years"; JBC papers, HUA I 5.168, "Widener Library, 1939-39" file.

Pages 116-117: "to improve conditions"; KDM papers, HUA III 50.8.11.3 box 46.

Pages 117-120: letters to and from staff in the service, ibid; Ira Steiner to KDM, ibid.

Page 122: "interested in it . . . unwilling to discard them"; KDM, *My Harvard Library Years*, page 62.

Page 124: "has been in the past"; ibid., pages 82-4.

Pages 124-125: "site that I wanted"; ibid.

Pages 125-126: "express your belief" and *The Open Shelf*; KDM papers, HUA III 50.8.11.3, box 46, "Lamont Library" file.

Page 126: "within the building"; ibid.

Page 128: "keep within bounds"; KDM, *HLB* volume 3 (1949), page 188.

Pages 129-130: "should be some solution"; KDM papers, HUA III 50.8.11.3, box 21, John Shea folder.

Page 130: "rapidly as possible"; memo to JS 5 dec. 1941, ibid.

Pages 130-131: "strenuous a summer"; AS to JS, 18 July 1950, ibid.

Page 131: "everywhere at once"; HUA, John Shea HUG biographical file.

Page 132: "laxative in your work"; John T. Bethell, Richard M. Hunt, and Robert Shenton, *Harvard A to Z* (Cambridge, MA: Harvard 2004), "Characters," pages 58-9.

Pages 133-135: "Harvard to support"; KDM papers, HUA III 50.8.11.3, box 45, "Service in Widener (& Complaints)" folder.

Pages 137-138: "rather than architectural"; KDM papers, HUA III 50.8.11.3 box 46, "Faculty Response to Proposal Article, 1949-50" folder.

Page 138: "Library have been"; KDM papers, 1 May 1952, HUA III 50.8.11.3.

Page 140: "rooms to study"; clipping in KDM papers, HUA III 50.8.11.3, box 20, "Communist Books in Local Libraries" file.

Page 141: "the stair landing"; Committee on Decorum 1958-60, HUA III 50.10.117.

Page 142: "perhaps a postwar phase"; ibid.

Page 142: "downfall of nations created"; Ernest Villas to Nathan Marsh Pusey, 2 January 1960; ibid.

Page 143-144: "present community standards"; Foster Palmer papers, Conditions in the Widener Reading Room, HUA III 50.10.10.3.

Page 145: "individual staff member"; HUA, Library, staff in the 1970s, memos and letters to Alan Erickson and D. Bryant on staff problems, 1971, HUA III 50.29.71. See also Morton Keller and Phyllis Keller, *Making Harvard Modern: the Rise of America's University* (New York and Oxford: Oxford 2001); Bethell, *Harvard Observed*.

Pages 146-147: "worse than I do" . . . "amount of money"; Houghton Library/Widener Memorial Rooms 1915-70, HUA III 50.8.119.50.5, "Gutenberg Bible" folder.

Page 149: "interrogate the memory unit"; Circulation Division, HUA III 50.8.114.10.

Page 150: OCLC and Fred Kilgour; Ken Carpenter, *First 350 Years of the Harvard University Library* (Cambridge, MA: Harvard University Library 1986), page 162.

Page 151: "full-sized paper copy"; Library, planning for future, 1966 HUA III 50.29.66 a,b.

Page 155: "slander to defend himself"; Jeffrey Nelson Book Theft Case, 1977, HUA III 50.29.77.59.

Page 160: "trek to make"; Jan Ziolkowski, *HLB* n.s. 6:3, Fall 1995, page 38.

Pages 160-163: for discussion of the library's automation, see Ken Carpenter, *350 Years*; see also Keller and Keller, *Making Harvard Modern*.

Page 164: "nation's scholarly resources"; Harvard College Library Departmental Annual Reports, 1985.

Page 165: "complex of networks"; Neil Rudenstine, AR 1991-3, page 59.

Page 168: for discussion of card catalogs see Nicholson Baker, "Discards," in *The Size of Thoughts: Essays and Other Lumber* (New York: Random House (1996).

Pages 168-171: my discussion of the planning and procedures of the Widener renovation is based on notes and documents held by the Harvard College Librarian's Office, as well as on discussions with Nancy Cline and Paul Bellenoit.

Pages 178-179: figures from Facilities Management Department, Harvard College Library.

Page 185: "disciplines in college curricula"; Oscar Handlin, *Truth in History*. New Brunswick, USA: Transaction, 1998, pages 58-9. "gray Ukrainian town"; Handlin, *The Uprooted* (Boston: Little, Brown 1951), page 322.

Image Credits

Unless otherwise noted below, images appear by courtesy of the Harvard University Archives.

title page: see page 81 photo credit below.
Pages xiv-xv: Gore Hall, 22 January 1913. Photograph by H. Robinson Shepherd. HUV 48 (20-9).
Page xvi: Gabriel Ferrier, portrait of Harry Elkins Widener, 1913. Photograph by Katya Kallsen. Courtesy of the Harvard University Portrait Collection, Gift of Eleanor Elkins Widener for the Widener Room, Widener Library, 1915.
Page 7: "Interior of the South Library looking from the South Door." dated 21 October 1912, gift of John S. Lawrence '71. HUA, HUV 48 (5-1).
Pages 8-9: Gore Hall shelf guide, HUA.
Page 10: William Coolidge Lane, ca. 1912. HUA, HUP Lane, William Coolidge (6b).
Page 12: from HUA, "1906: Library plans, papers of Mr. Lane"; HUA III 29.06.3.
Page 13: HUA, HUP Eliot, Charles W. (6a).
Page 14: Cast picture of HEW from Scrapbook of N.C. Nash, HUA, HUD 907.58f.
Page 15: photograph of books in the HEW collection by Stephen Sylvester and Bob Zinck, HCL Imaging Services. The books include, from top, HEW 6.7.7, *The Letters of John Keats to Fanny Brawne . . .* (London, Reeves & Turner, 1878 [i.e. 1888]); HEW 8.1.2, William Morris, *The Defence of Guenevere and Other Poems* (Hammersmith: Kelmscott, 1892); HEW 8.1.3, William Morris, *The Earthly Paradise*, vols. 1-3 (Hammersmith: Kelmscott, 1896-7); HEW 9.13.15 F, Thomas Rowlandson (1756-1827), 75 original drawings and studies in watercolor; HEW 4.12.6 PF, George Cruikshank, Caricatures and other separate prints by George Cruikshank . . . the collection formed by Captain Douglas. Courtesy of Houghton Library of the Harvard College Library.
Page 17: HUA, HUP Coolidge, Archibald Cary (7a).
Page 24: HUA, HUP Coolidge, Archibald Cary (5a).
Page 25: HUA, HUP Widener-Rice, Eleanor Elkins (1).
Page 26: ca. 1925. HUA HUP Lowell, Abbott Lawrence (7b).
Page 31: HUA III 50.29.12.3.

Page 32: "Shooting books out of Gore Hall. 1912-13." HUA, HUV 48 (17-1).
Page 38: Widener plans. HUA III 50.8.12.3.
Page 39: Widener plans. HUA III 50.8.12.3.
Page 40: "The Widener Library under construction, 4 December 1913." HUV 49 (25-5).
Page 44, top: postcard from the private collection of David Whitesell.
Page 44, bottom: photo by Paul J. Weber, n.d. HUV 49 (18-2).
Page 49: John Downame, *The Christian Warfare Against the Devill World and Flesh...* London: Printed by William Stansby, 1634.
Pages 50-1: HUV 49 (19-9a).
Page 52: *Harvard Illustrated Magazine*, June 1915. HUA, HUK 462.
Page 54: HUV 49 (13-2).
Page 57: HUV 49 (12-3).
Page 58: HUV 49 (14-16).
Page 59: Photo by [Paul J.?] Weber. "Neg. #156." HUV 49 (6-2).
Page 62: *Harvard Crimson*, 27 September 1918, page 3.
Page 63, top: John Singer Sargent, *Gassed mustard gas, the dressing station at Le Bae-de-Sud on Doullens-Arras Road August 1918*. Courtesy of the Art Archive and the Imperial War Museum, ref: AA332861.
Page 63: bottom: John Singer Sargent, Studies of Three Soldiers with Rifles, Arms Extended, for "Coming of the Americans," Widener Library, Harvard University, 1921-22. Courtesy of the Fogg Art Museum, Harvard University, Art Museums, Gift of John Singer Sargent.
Pages 64-5: John Singer Sargent, *Death and Victory* (left) and *Coming of the Americans* or *Entering the War* (right), Widener Library, 1922. Photograph by David Remington, Stephen Sylvester, and Bob Zinck.
Page 68 top: Farnsworth Collection bookplate, HUA III 150.15.141A.
Page 68 bottom: Farnsworth Room postcard, HUA III 150.15.141.
Page 71: sketch in Farnsworth scrapbook, HUA III 150.15.141B.
Page 73: Widener stack, 29 June 1915. HUV 49 (14-4a). Boston Photo News Co., Fine money.
Page 77: Widener ground floor. HUV 49 (10-8). Harvard Film Service #409.
Page 81 and title page: "January 27 at the beginning of the reading period." HUV 49 (15-6).
Page 91: Harvard Film Service 406. HUV 49 (4-5).
Page 94: Harvard Film Service, 1946. HUV 49 (18-5).
Page 97: HUP Metcalf, Keyes Dewitt (9a). n.d.
Page 99: 1946. HUV 49 (8-3).
Page 100: UAIII 50. 15.140.10A.
Page 109: Currier, T.F. Chart of Classification and cataloging . . . processes. HUA III 50.29.36.16.
Page 112: HUA III 50.15.140H.
Page 113: HUV 49 (10-6).
Page 121: KDM papers and correspondence, HUA III 50.8.11.3, box 46, Widener staff in service.

Page 126: Coolidge, Shepley, Bulfinch, and Abbot, Architects, rendering of the Lamont Browsing Room, n.d. [ca. 1948]. KDM papers and correspondence, HUA III 50.8.11.3, box 46, Lamont Library file.
Page 127: *The Open Shelf*, June 1948. KDM papers and correspondence, HUA III 50.8.11.3, box 46, Lamont Library file.
Page 132: John Shea, ca. 1937. HUG 4775.
Page 135: KDM papers and correspondence, HUA III 50.8.11.3, box 45, Widener rehab–lighting.
Page 136: Widener News Office. HUV 49 (6-5).
Pages 152-3: Courtesy of HCL Communications.
Page 154: Courtesy of HCL Communications. Photograph by Paula Carter.
Page 169: Courtesy of HCL Communications.
Page 172: Courtesy of HCL Communications.
Page 176: Courtesy of HCL Communications.
Page 177: Courtesy of HCL Communications.
Page 180: Courtesy of Harvard News Office. Photograph by Justin Ide.
Page 181 top and bottom: Courtesy of HCL Communications.
Page 182: Courtesy of HCL Communications.
Page 183: Courtesy of HCL Communications.
Page 185: Courtesy of Harvard News Office. Photograph by Kris Snibbe.

Index

Abele, Julian Francis 27-8
American Institute of Architects 28
American Library Association in World War One 76; Cataloging Code Committee 110; Victory Book Campaign (World War Two) 122
Andover Library 30
Andrews, C.W. 38
Annual Report 6, 101, 102, 156, 165
Appleton Chapel 2
Aras, Vito 146, 148, 156, 169; see burglaries and thefts
automation 149-51, 157-63, 165, 168
backlog, cataloging 159, 164
Bacon Francis, *Essais* 16
Baker, Nicholson 168
Bellenoit, Paul 171, 178
Bentinck-Smith, William 6
Billings, J.C. 11
  see New York Public Library
Black, Alistair 2
Blake, Robert Pierpont 89
Bok, Derek 156, 157
Bond, Richard 4; see Gore Hall
book, future of the 151, 165
Boston Evening Transcript 28, 89
Boston Herald 131
Boston Post 88, 139
Boston Public Library 118, 141
Briggs, L.B.R. 30
Briggs, William Benjamin 90
Buck, Paul H. 115, 138-9
Bundy, McGeorge 138
Bunting, Bainbridge 5
burglaries and thefts 59, 88-9, 146, 155-6
Bush, Douglas 105
canonical library collections 20, 148
Carnegie, Andrew 13
Carney, Frank; and James Russell Lowell 2; childhood 3; and John Langdon Sibley 3-4; and Henry Wadsworth Longfellow 4; as stack boy 4; knowledge of collections 6; and book moves *31*, 31-5, 48, 171; and electric trucks 46; and Widener opening 53; and working life of Widener 55; chairs and tables 56; troubles with building 58-60, 74; and elevators 76, 178; and labor difficulties 76-7; and burglaries and thefts 59, 88; and John Shea 129-32; and Paul Bellenoit 178
Carpenter, Kenneth E. 164, 171
cataloging and classification; in Gore Hall 6; under T. Frank Currier 108-9; and NEDL 123; costs associated with duplicate catalogs 137, see Union and Public catalogs; LC and Widener systems 158-60
Chest of 1900 3
Chicago, University of 61
Cline, Nancy 168, *169*, 177, 178
Cold War, the 139
Commencement 47-8, 139
Communist books 139-40
Conant, James Bryant; meritocratic ideals 69; and A. Lawrence Lowell 91-3; and change 102-4, 138-9; and refugee scholars 116; and Red Book 124; and Lamont Library 124-5; as High Commissioner to Germany 141; pragmatic approach to knowledge 148
Conlan, Milda E. 115, see tea
Coolidge, Archibald Cary; early career 16-7; *17*; Hohenzollern Collection 17; and *Kulturgeschichte* 19; and research library 20; managerial style 22; and A. L. Lowell 23; new library plans 23-7; *24*; relations with faculty 28-30; and book moves 30-3, 170; Widener plans 35-41; and reception of Widener 45; at open-

ing of Widener 48; collecting for World War One 61; and studies 72-5; retirement 89; library centralization 94; and K.D. Metcalf 97-8, 128; and composite nature of Widener 103; and Widener classification system 158
Corporation, the Harvard 11-2, 29, 96, 118, 125, 155
crane, construction *176*, 177
Cranston, Arnold B. *71*
Currier, Margaret 117, see tea
Currier, T. Frank 108-110, 113, 129
custodes librorum 2
D-Day 118
"dead books" 108, 122, 163
Decorum Committee 141
Deed of Trust 41-2
De Genarro, Richard 150, 165, 167
Dewey Decimal System 158
discipline 78-87
Distributable Union Catalog (DUC) 161-2, 165
Dixon, Eleanor Widener 170
Downame, John's *Christian Warfare* 48, *49*
ductwork 179
Economics, Law, and Political Science Reading Room 80
Einhorn, Yaffee, Prescott 168
Eisenhower, Dwight D. 139
electrical system 179
Eliot, Charles William; *13*; appointment 10; and library 10-13, 123; retirement 13, 16; and A. L. Lowell 23; turn to research and professionalism 61; and "dead books" 108, 122, 163
Emerton, Ephraim 19-20, 28, 72, 75
endowment, Harvard 13, 92, *157*
Fainsod, Merle 150-1
Farmington Plan, the 128
Farnsworth, Henry Weston 67-9
Farnsworth, Lucy 69
Farnsworth Room, the 67-72

"fixed shelf" system 6; *8-9*; see also cataloging and classification
Foreign Affairs 17
Fox, John 140
fresh flowers 42, 70
Gatsos, John Dimitrios 129
Gilded Age, the 13, 14, 18, 21, 61
Gitlin, Todd 144
Gleason, John 119
Goodman, Benny 120
Gore Hall [*ii*]; [*xiv-xv*]; 2; paging books in 4; design 4-5; stack 6, 41; replacement of 10, 23, 28; conditions in 6, 20, 22; proposed additions to *12*; moving out of 30-5, *32*; as site of Widener 41; loss 4; demolition of 46; finials *154*
Grieder, Elmer 118
Guastavino, Rafael Jr., *77*
Gutenberg Bible 15, 16, 120; theft attempt 145, 156, see Aras, Vito; effect on public imagination 146-8
Handlin, Oscar 163, 185-7
Hart, Albert Bushnell 45
Harvard Crimson, the 62, 80, 86, 98, 100, 104-5
Harvard Depository (HD) 163-5; and HD Push 171; and Oscar Handlin 186-7
Harvard Graduates' Magazine, the 18, 19
Harvard Illustrated Magazine, the 52
Harvard, John 48
Harvard Monthly, the 100
Harvard Theatre Collection 120
Harvard Union (library) 94, and house libraries 101
Hayden, Tom 144
Haynes, Ralph 133, 141
Hellenic Chronicle, the 142
Hibbard, Laura A. 111
Hofer, Philip 90
Hohenzollern Collection 17
HOLLIS (Harvard On-Line Library

Information System) 160-2, 165, 168, 171
Houghton, Arthur 124
Houghton Library 10, 90, 95, 108, 124, 128, 138, 147, 164
humanities and social sciences 95, 107, 132; see also book, future of the; canonical library collections; Ziolkowski, Jan
Huntington, Henry Edwards 16
IBM 1401 computer 150
ice cream 42
"Inferno" case 35
in loco parentis 83, 100
Jackson, William A. 90
James, Henry 5-6, 70-1
John Crerar Library 38
Johns Hopkins University 61
Jones, Howard Mumford 133, 137
Keough, Francis 117
Kilgour, Fred 150
Knowles, Jeremy 168
Kress Library 164
kulturgeschichte see Coolidge, Archibald Cary
labor unrest 76, see also Carney, Frank
Lamont Library 30, 95, 108, 124-8
Lamont, Thomas 124-5
Lamson, Peggy 131
Lane, William Coolidge, and library needs 6-11; *10*; and collections 18, and A.C. Coolidge 22, on move out of Gore 34, on Widener plans 35-41, 46, on Widener opening 53, and memorials 63, retirement 90, as scholar-librarian 129; see also discipline
Larson, Henrietta M. 113 see also women in the library
Lee Kennedy Company 168
library as construction site 171-8
Library Journal 34, 53, 61, 72
library *qua* laboratory 19
Lichtenstein, Walter 18, 19, 21, 46

lighting 95, 98, 101, 133, 135-6, 179
Littauer Library 107
Lodge, Henry Cabot 46, 66
Loker, Katherine B. 183
Longfellow, Henry Wadsworth 4
Lowell, A. Lawrence and CWE, 13; and endowment 13; agenda 16, and ACC 23, 30, 31; fundraising 23; and Eleanor Elkins Widener 42-3; and Widener plans 37, 40, 43, 45-6; and stack 56; and World War One 60, 66; and John Singer Sargent 62-6
Lowell, James Russell, see Carney, Frank
Lowell, Reverend William 23
Lower Reading Room, see Economics, Law, and Political Science Reading Room
Lynnewood Hall 25
MARC (Machine Readable Catalog Record) 150, 159-62
Marshall, George 139
Martin, Louis 155
McCarthy, Senator Joseph 139
McNamara, Robert 144
Memorial Church 1
Memorial Stadium 30
Metcalf, Keyes Dewitt appointment 90; first professional librarian at Harvard 93; and specialization 94; and James Bryant Conant 94; Widener space 95; and research library 95; struggle with Widener building 95-6; early life 96; growth and expansion of library 96-99; reform of Widener 99-108; and T. Frank Currier 108-9; and women in the library 111-16; and refugee scholars 116-20; and son Gerry 118; and Benny Goodman 120; and NEDL 122-4, 163; and Lamont Library 124-8; and the library profession 128-9; and John Shea 129-30; alterations to

Index 199

Widener 133-6; and merger of Union and Public Catalogues 137-8; and McGeorge Bundy 138; and light courts 169; and mezzanine proposal 137, 184
Milner, Florence 69-72
Milton, John 46-7
Moody, Roland 117, 119
Morgan, J.P. 23
Morrison, Samuel Eliot 60
Morrison, Theodore 106
Morizé, Andre 105
nouveau-riche, the 14, 27
Murdock, Kenneth B. 105
Museum of Fine Arts, the 66
mythology of Widener 42
Nelson, Jeffrey 155, see burglaries and thefts
NEDL (New England Depository Library) 108, 122-3, 128, 163
New Yard 1
New York Public Library 11, 13, 90 see also Billings, J. C.
Oberlin College 96, see also KDM
OCLC (Online Computer Library Center) 150, 157-8, 162
Olmsted, Frederick Law 5
Open Shelf, the 125, *127*
Owen, Wilfred 67
Palmer, Foster 150
Pisani, Assunta 163-4
Potter, A[lfred] C[laghorn] 90
Prall, D. W. 105
Public Catalog 137; see KDM, merger of Union and Public Catalogs
Pusey Library 160, 173
Pusey, Nathan Marsh 138, 141, 142, 145
Putnam, Herbert 45
Quaritch book shop 16
Quincy, Josiah 4
Radcliffe Reading Room 36-7, 87, 114; see also women in the library
Rand, Benjamin 29
Randall Hall 30-5, 41, 46, 48
Rare Books Annex 124; see also Houghton Library
Red Book, the; see Conant, James Bryant
refugee scholars 116
reserve books 36, 40, 55, 78, 80, 82, 84, 85, 98, 105-6, 131, 133, 137
Rinker, Catherine C. 116; see tea
Rollins, Hyder 178
Root, Anna Metcalf (KDM's sister) 96
Root, Azariah Smith (KDM's brother-in-law) 96
Rosenbach, A. S. W. 15
ROTC 144
Rowe, Addie Francis 178
Rudenstine, Neil 157, 165, 168
Sargent, John Singer 63-6
Schlesinger, Arthur Jr. 131
Scientific American 13
Shea, John 117, 129-33, *132*
Sibley, John Langdon 2-4
signage 173-4
Social Relations, Department of 144
soil removal 179
staff in war service 60, 117-20, *121*
Steiner, Ira 120
Stoddard, Roger E. 147
Students for a Democratic Society (SDS) 144-8, 149
studies 19, 36-7, 40, 72-6, 78, 131, 137, 170, 174
swim test, see mythology
Tesler, Ron 171
Titanic, the 16, 21, 23, 25, 47, 63
Treasure Room 35, 36, 90, *91*, 116, 170, 180
Trumbauer, Horace 25, 27-8, 35-8, 40-1, 43, 98, 103
Union Catalog 110, 134, 137; see also Public Catalog; KDM, merger of Union and Public Catalogs
University Hall takeover 144-5; library staff reaction to 145
Vanserg Hall 155
Veblen, Thorstein 20-1, 61, 93, 139, 148

Victory Book Campaign, see
 American Library Association
Villas, Ernest 142
"V-mail" 117, *121*
wages 55, 76-8, 96, 101, 109, 137
Warren, H. C. 18
Weinberger, Arnold 116
Wendell, Barrett 43
Weyand, Johnny 171
Whitman, Walt 47
Widener (Rice), Eleanor Elkins 14-5, *25*, 25-7, 41-6, 63, 90, 169
Widener, George 25
Widener, George D. 170
Widener, Harry Elkins [*xvi*], 14 (illus), 14-6, 25, 26, 42, 46, 63, 67, 68, 88, 120, 121, 170, 180
Widener Library, plans, *38*, *39*; exterior views *44*, *50-51*, *52*, *62*, *94*, *152-153*, *154*, *176*; interior views *54*, *57*, *58*, *59*, *64*, *65*, *68*, *73*, *77*, *81*, *91*, *113*, *135*, *136*, *172*, *177*, *180*, *181*, *182*, *183*
Widener, P. A. B. 14, 16, 120
Wiener, Leo 18
Williams, Edwin E. 96
Williams, Joel Clifton 88-9; see burglaries and thefts
Winship, George Parker 42-3, 90
Winsor, Justin 5-6, 129
Wittlesley, Derwent 106
Wood, Marilyn 171
women in the library, difficulties faced by 36-7, 55, 76-8, 86-7, 108-16, 128
Work, Robert L. 118
World Wide Web 162
Ziolkowski, Jan 160

THE TYPEFACE
in which the text of this book is set was named after Justus Erich Walbaum (1768-1859?), who apprenticed as a maker of confectionary molds before becoming a punchcutter and printer. While neoclassical in intent, Walbaum captures the dark aspect of machine-set type in use at the time Widener was built. Its designer is Frantisek Storm. The caption face is Scala Sans, a calligraphic sans serif designed by Martin Majoor; the titles are rendered in Carol Twombly's Trajan, which closely matches the capitals found on Widener's entablature. This book was designed on a Macintosh computer in the author's office in Houghton Library, Harvard University, and was printed by The Stinehour Press in Lunenburg, Vermont.